Ralph Hamilton
1974–2002

TELL MY MOTHER I'M NOT DEAD

A CASE STUDY IN MEDIUMSHIP RESEARCH

TREVOR HAMILTON

imprint-academic.com

Copyright © Trevor Hamilton, 2012

The moral rights of the author have been asserted.
No part of this publication may be reproduced in any form
without permission, except for the quotation of brief passages
in criticism and discussion.

Published in the UK by
Imprint Academic, PO Box 200, Exeter EX5 5YX, UK

Published in the USA by
Imprint Academic, Philosophy Documentation Center
PO Box 7147, Charlottesville, VA 22906-7147, USA

ISBN 9781845402600

A CIP catalogue record for this book is available from the
British Library and US Library of Congress

For Anne, Dan, and Ralph

Contents

Introduction	1
Part 1: Experiences	4
Part 2: Reflections	86
Part 3: Conclusions	154
Appendix 1: Analysis of Results	164
Appendix 2: Predictive Statements and their Status	166
Appendix 3: Glossary	170
Resources and references	176

Introduction

This short book divides into two parts. The first section is a personal narrative of the impact of the death of our son Ralph on us and our efforts to see if there was any evidence for his continued existence (generated largely through visits to mediums) that a grieving but thinking person could take seriously. The second section is an attempt to evaluate objectively (so far as that is possible for people in our position) the quality of that evidence and to come to some conclusion.

Both parts are necessary in order to do justice to the complexity and intensity of the subject matter. The title *Tell My Mother I'm Not Dead: A Case Study in Mediumship Research* is meant to reflect the dual nature of this book: recognition of the incredibly powerful and persuasive nature of the language often used in a sitting with a medium, and the need always to test this language against objective and scientific criteria.

Others were strongly affected by Ralph's death, as well as ourselves: Dan his older brother, Ralph's girlfriend, and his many friends. I have not included their experiences in this short book; except very briefly, out of respect for their privacy, but we both fully acknowledge what they, too, must have suffered. No matter how intense and private our grief, we constantly reminded ourselves that Dan had lost his only sibling, someone who had been part of his life from birth, and part of his very identity.

I have spent a considerable (perhaps an over-indulgent) amount of time on my thought processes and emotions in the first part. I did this because I wanted the reader to experience the turmoil I was going through and my fear, at times, that I was not judging things objectively because of weaknesses in my own personality. I have also given space to what was possibly a mildly paranoid sequence of events, since to delete it would not be honest, and in fact it had, for me at least, interesting insights into the nature of evidence and truth and the way in which individuals construct their view of reality.

The second part of the book seeks to evaluate the sessions with mediums on the basis of some of the small but significant research that has taken in several different centres across the world. The book is subtitled 'a case study' since it is the record of a set of individual experiences outside a controlled environment. Yet, real-world studies are as important as laboratory work in order to try to understand the conditions and processes under which such phenomena may or may not take place.

I have provided pretty full accounts of the statements every medium made so that each reader can judge the situation for themselves, and one recurring theme through the book is the need for individuals and parapsychologists to engage directly with this most central of issues—the hypothesis of the survival of bodily death and the search for high quality evidence from competent, well-trained mediums to confirm or deny this.

Because the book covers both individual experience and issues involved in assessing such experiences objectively, it is hoped that it will help those who have suffered loss and who, given some initial support and guidance, would wish to embark on the same journey I have made. This book may also provide parapsychologists with some future research perspectives, but it has been written primarily for a more general audience and I make no claim to highly specialised expertise. The section on the variety and range of types of evidence for life after death, for example, is indicative of the material available and certainly not a comprehensive account.

If the reader wishes to pursue the matters and issues outlined in this book in greater detail, she/he could do no better than join the Society for Psychical Research. I have found those members of that society, whom I have come to know, highly intelligent, helpful, and well balanced individuals. They give the complete lie to the old canard that people interested in this field are dotty, vague, and impractical. They are some of the sharpest people I have met. In addition, the electronic online library that membership gives access to is a hugely valuable resource for further investigation and research.

Finally, I would like to thank Anne and Dan for their loving support during the writing of this book, and all those others who have made useful and helpful comments on it.

Note 1: I have used words like extrasensory perception, psi, super-psi as more or less equivalent and as describing the unknown force or forces generating anomalous or paranormal phenomena. I have not always been consistent in attaching 'alleged', 'ostensible', and 'apparent' to these terms. One should not read into this inconsistency either whole-hearted belief or disbelief in the events and experiences outlined. I have also included a glossary of terms (Appendix 3) of some of the more unfamiliar terms — to a reader new to this subject — that have been used in this book.

Note 2: I reference books/articles that have helped form my views by author, and date of edition used (and also by page where appropriate). Details of all articles, books, and websites consulted are given at the end of this publication.

PART 1
Experiences

2002

July

If a Mr and Mrs Hamilton are on board, would they please remain seated till the other passengers have left.

The plane had just landed at Bristol on a dull afternoon. We had returned from a week's holiday in Paris. Anne and I looked at each other.

Perhaps it's your mother. Maybe it's the car.

But we knew it had to be something more significant than that: something to do with our sons, Dan or Ralph.

We sat and sat. One man took ages, fussily adjusting his dress, and checking and rechecking his bag. Eventually we made the exit. All the stewardess, with her bright professional smile, could say was that she didn't know what it was all about, but the police would like to talk to us. A pleasant but unsmiling policewoman, with a large guy in plain clothes beside her, stood at the bottom of the steps.

Yes, we were Mr and Mrs Hamilton. Yes, Ralph did drive a car with that number plate.

Is it Ralph? Is it Ralph?

We said that again and again as we walked with them into the terminal. But she merely replied that she wanted us to identify some items—and we did—in a small airless room just off the passenger check in.

Yes, that was his watch given to him by the girl who had nearly broken his heart. Yes, yes, yes (hurriedly to get it over with) to all the other effects. Everything was just plain unreal, as if we were being forced to take part in a film and speak lines that referred to the tragedies of other people. I wanted to stop the kind police woman and say, OK, I realise you are just doing your job, but you've got the wrong parents.

Then she told us the details.

We soon realised why she had initially refused to answer our questions. She first wanted to establish that Ralph was the driver, because the driver of that car had been in a fatal accident (a collision with a bus at 12.45 on the outskirts of a West Country town on Sunday July 7th — our last day in Paris). Anne, curiously enough, had experienced at that time a brief, terrible sense of desolation, and had to get up off the bench, as we sat dozing in the sunlight in the Jardin du Luxembourg, and just move around for a few minutes. The mood soon faded as we left the gardens and encountered thousands of brightly dressed roller skaters speeding down the streets specially closed for them each Sunday.

The policewoman was very kind but also very professional. As she drove us home (we were not allowed to drive our own car) I saw her watching us in the mirror, scanning our faces for any clues as to possible reasons for his death.

July 8th

Once home the next horror was checking the phone messages and hearing Ralph's girlfriend's voice — she had obviously rung several times — asking Ralph why he wouldn't answer. Apart from our grief, we had to remember what she had suffered. She told us later that she had arranged to come to our house on the evening of the 7th of July to dinner with Ralph and stay with him overnight. She arrived but there was no one to let her in. She waited and waited. Our neighbour next door came out to talk to her. The neighbour knew what had happened since the police had already been round to try to trace us, but she could not tell the girl in case it had not been Ralph driving the car. She went home and her father rang all the hospitals but to no avail. Her sad, anguished voice resonated on the answerphone.

Ralph, are you there, why won't you answer, what is going on? Please contact me.

We identified Ralph's body at a local hospital. We could only look at him through a window. Insanely, I felt that if we refused to look we could somehow turn the clock back and not be forced to take part in a play we hadn't written and would never have wanted to write. We would not be grieving parents. Ralph would not be dead. But we had to look.

It was him and wasn't him and there was a bruise on his face.

The supervisor accompanying us was what they called in the West Country, a good old boy. He was well-meaning but started to patronise Anne and call her mother.

Get mother out soon. Mother doesn't want to have too much of this. Mother can't go in.

Anne said afterwards that if he didn't stop saying mother, mother would bloody well thump him.

We spent the next three days in bed, cold and stunned with grief and clinging to each other. Monday and Tuesday and Wednesday, the 8th, 9th, and 10th of July 2002. As we lay there I suddenly remembered a visit I had made, on the spur of the moment, to a medium the previous March.

I had walked past the sign in the city centre many times before. It was obvious and a bit crude and reminded me of fairground fortune tellers and top-of-the-pier palmists. It pointed inwards towards the local covered market which I sometimes used for food shopping. I'd go to the Country Farmers' Wives' stall and buy their cheese or their robust, earthy bread and pasties. The market was a mixture of these jolly rural ladies and slightly miserable looking stallholders selling junk or memorabilia that was only one notch up from the average charity shop. But that day somewhere in March 2002, on impulse, prompted by a board advertising *Psychic Readings*, I went straight across the floor to the tiny cubicle where the readings, apparently, took place.

I had always been interested in the paranormal, finding the bland Anglicanism of my upbringing unsatisfactory for a variety of reasons. Every few years I would suddenly dive into a shop for a tarot reading or consult a medium just to see if there was anything in it. In my own life I had occasionally experienced odd, so-called supernatural events — precognitive dreams, a frightening experience with the Ouija board when a student, vaguely poltergeist activity in adolescence — and I always promised myself that one day when I had time I would systematically investigate the area.

So in I went. The psychic was a solidly built man in a wheelchair, and as I met him I realised that I had dreamt this encounter before. I was in a room with a man in a wheelchair and he was telling me something frightening and threatening that would have severe consequences for me. There was also, in the dream, an African sculpture which startled me. There was no such sculpture in this work space.

Rubbish, rubbish, rubbish.

So said the rational sergeant major in my head to all this mumbo jumbo.

His wife, or partner, was blonde and thin. She was a rather wispy presence who, after lighting some incense, moved behind a curtain to deeper in the room. I was not sure I liked him. He made a slightly sarcastic comment about the softness of my hands, read my palm, did some numerology, and gave me numbers for the lottery. That irritated me and I said so. I rather pompously saw myself as a serious seeker after truth. But, he said, most people liked getting them. Is this all it is then, I thought, just a line of giggly bank holiday people after future lottery or pools or racing tips?

Then he became very serious.

There is a lot of spirit activity around you at the moment. There is a burden you will have to bear and you will bear it. I see a red-haired woman in spirit. You will shortly come into a lump sum. You have strong visualisation skills and could develop as a medium. I think you might well write about this one day.

After some inconsequential chat, and his moan about the positioning of his sign and his not being publicised enough, I left, clutching my numerology chart and feeling cheated. But beneath my irritation prickled the menace of my dream about the man in the wheelchair who would do me harm. As I left he asked if I lived locally and he seemed a little stunned, even exhausted. I could see no relevance in any of his statements. I had taken early retirement — there was, alas, no more lump sum to come, and my wife had already retired. I could remember no red-haired women living or dead. And what was this burden? It was all far too vague and generalised. The memory of the dream and the threat faded and if there was a burden to come, it very probably referred to the death of my mother-in-law who was in her nineties.

Yet, over this year information contained in my dream and given at his sitting was confirmed. The day before Ralph died we had been in the Pompidou Centre riding up the transparent cylindrical escalators to the top floor where the permanent art exhibition was. As I turned, in that vague, slightly stupefied way one sometimes does in art galleries (or at least I do) I had recoiled, suddenly glimpsing a ferocious African artefact exhibited close beside me. It was as if, in my dream, I had collected, in advance, psychic fragments associated with the context of Ralph's death. But that was absurd wasn't it?

But that was not all. Just before we went on holiday I had walked past Ralph's bedroom to my study and it suddenly hit me

He is going to die and you are going to write about it.

It was such a horrible thought that I quickly dismissed it. I had not been getting on with the personal writing that I wanted to and so I rationalised the incident by arguing that, at some stratum in my mind, I realised that I needed a shock to galvanise me into action, and this was the hideous thing that my subconscious mind came up with: that it was really a statement to the effect that only something major would motivate me, rather than a prediction of something that was going to happen.

July 18th

When I retired we moved to a quiet and attractive village a few miles outside the county capital. On the day of the funeral we walked, shielded from the sun by the scented conifers on the footpath, straight to the church without having to go along on the main road. It was a footpath we had delighted in when we first came to the village. It had fields of maize on one side and, on the other, lyrical views across the valley of grazing cattle and down at the river, kingfishers and herons, cygnets and swans. It was almost too sweet and unbearable an English pastoral. Yet, through such a scene, in bright sun (the fact that he died in an unusually glorious summer made it even more tragic) went Anne and I, Dan, our eldest son, and Ralph's girlfriend, all taut and dapper in our funeral clothes.

The experience was wonderful and nerve-wracking at the same time. Anne had made a friend in the village (at that time her hair was tinted red), who had a personal and an academic interest in community arts and practice. She worked with Anne to decorate the coffin. It took the form of a tree of life branching out from Ralph and attached to each branch were photos of different stages in his life. Anne's friend had allowed the coffin to be laid out in a beautiful room in her house which had a splendid polished wooden floor and historic panelling. Her enthusiasm to enrich his rite of passage, and the lovely temporary setting for the coffin, did not diminish the pain but washed some of the bleakness out of it. And the scale of the images and illustrations of his young life meant that during the funeral service he was celebrated within the environment of the church but the church did not take over and swamp his identity and uniqueness with its sometimes mechanical ritual. The young priest in charge of the parish understood this perfectly but unfortunately he was away and the service was conducted by his deputy, a heavily built, semi-retired vicar of the old school who, having been given his orders by his superior, tried his best to conform, but could not help his traditional views, and a recognisable type of Anglican pomposity, coming through at times.

A tall, thoughtful friend of Ralph's from the music world, crouched by the choir stall, ready to play Ralph's music as the coffin and the pall-bearers entered. I read some poetry, and Anne, Dan, and Ralph's girlfriend paid their tributes. None of us faltered, all went well, even the vicar lost that faint sense of being a professional amongst amateurs, and, to Ralph's music, we went out to bury Ralph, wrapped in his grandmother's shawl, in a grave that Anne would later turn into a pretty grave/garden of flowers and shrubs.

We then went the few yards across to the pub. The church had been full, to our surprise, and very largely composed of Ralph's friends who had come from all corners of the country and beyond. We had no idea that he had been so popular, so liked, so loved, as became evident while we drank, ate, and half laughed and cried through that long, sunlit afternoon.

A few days later I came up the stairs, a fair bit of wine inside me, and went into Ralph's room, left untouched — for even to glance in was to start up great pain — and said to him that I would find him wherever he had gone. And I tried to send him love, great waves of unconditional love to float him onwards, since I felt (we both did), from what folklore memory trace or B-movie I do not know, that we did not want to hold him back through the self-absorption of our grief.

August

But how was I to find him? Where was I to look? Who could I turn to for advice? How could I be sure that grief and loss hadn't weakened my judgment? And what did finding him actually mean? I started by looking back over my own life and I listed, first of all, events that I had long since thrust into the back of my mind:

- My mother told me that on the night of her father's death (she knew he was ill but not that he was near death), as she lay in bed his face came towards her and then receded
- She also stated that in a tea room in Wales, a spoon jumped in the air from her cup, a knife vibrated loudly without being hit, and a saucer smashed in front of her for no physical reason
- One of my sisters asserted that her husband promised that he would come back to her when he died and that one night she saw him at the end of the bed. She shouted go away, and he did in a brief, powerful explosion of energy
- One of my brothers twice encountered our deceased father on the landing of our family home
- Shortly after my father's death I was in our kitchen and for no reason a knife on one of the kitchen work surfaces suddenly spun round like a top for fifteen or twenty seconds
- As an adolescent and into my early twenties, as I stated earlier, I had experienced a number of odd semi-poltergeist type activities and one unpleasant experience at the Ouija board involving a friend.

So, was there an extra dimension to life beyond the material? These were people I loved and trusted (even though we were very different in character and interests). They had no history of mental illness nor any reason for wanting to draw attention to themselves. In fact, the only one I was suspicious of was the last on the list, me.

I had always been interested in the paranormal and had read quite widely, but not particularly discriminatingly, in that field over the years. I was worried that I might be led astray by a mixture of over-imagination and wishful thinking if I started my quest — however that might shape up — without guidance and structure. So, in what might seem rather a cold-blooded way, I developed a strategy which would give me structure and guidance and prevent me from deluding myself. I would join the Society for Psychical Research (the oldest and most prestigious organisation working in this field in the UK), I would read all I could on the history of the subject and, informed by this reading, I would visit a number of mediums to see if there was anything in it at all. As I was semi-retired (and then a few years later completely retired from salaried employment), and for years had been eager to do my own writing and research (rather than the turgid managerial prose I had to churn out in a number of my jobs), I decided to write the first biography of one of the leading figures in the founding and development of that society. This was F.W.H. Myers. He was a charismatic and brilliant figure in late-Victorian culture and society but is now largely forgotten, unlike his friends and contemporaries, George Eliot and John Ruskin (amongst others), who thought very highly of him.

I had an even more profound reason for my investigation. The impact of Ralph's death was absolutely devastating on Anne. She bore it very bravely and showed great courage in those early months. She had always had, she said, a peasant mentality in these matters (only what I can see, only what I can touch), and was very suspicious of mediumship and did not share my interest in the paranormal. I, therefore, hoped, in a way that I couldn't articulate at this stage, that something might come out of my search that would bring her comfort. So, she agreed, rather tentatively, that if I set it up, she would come with me to visit a medium or sensitive or psychic or whatever they were called.

Anne had no interest in the research side. She just wanted to know that Ralph was safe and not suffering. Her pain was, in some ways, worse than mine. She and Ralph had been very close when he was a child and she found his distancing from her, with the onset of adolescence, difficult to take. He, naturally, grew a shell to help him establish his individuality. And she felt she was losing him. However, just before his death, they had started coming back to each other, and this second withdrawal of intimacy was particularly hard to bear.

I was stimulated in my research by a number of strange phenomena that happened in the house in the weeks and months after his death. The television set in the kitchen came on by itself. Could that happen normally? The expensive Bose CD player and radio that Ralph liked so much and that had played his music at the funeral increased suddenly and then decreased in volume by itself. Could that happen normally? I started to dream vividly about him, first in a hospital situation in distress. He arched up from the bed and gently subsided as helpers gathered round him. That dream shook me and I prayed that he would be healed and reconciled to his new situation. Anne, to her distress, did not dream of him at all. But she did get an almost overwhelming sense of his presence at least twice in the house; and on several occasions she smelt his cigarette smoke. It was quite distinct from wood smoke. I smelt it too on a number of occasions, but I had to say

But we live in wood burning stove land. How can you be sure?

Obviously, in a rather fraught and superstitious way, I hoped that all of this meant that Ralph was trying to communicate with us. But I had to be on my guard against delusion. I met a woman who had lost her son and she told me that he made contact by dimming the lights and by wispy, cobwebby touches to her face. I inwardly scoffed at that, but as I went to the lavatory in the middle of the night (the familiar pilgrimage of the late middle-aged man), I began to notice a flickering of blue-white light in the bulb after I switched the landing light off—the light outside Ralph's bedroom. Sometimes it blazed quite powerfully. During the day I tested it several times, closing the curtains. Never once did switching it off produce the same effect as at night. The obvious conclusion was that it was a faulty switch. Yet, if this was the case, why didn't it happen during the day? Anne said that it was just a dodgy switch. An electrician, in the house one day on another job, could not come up with an explanation.

My first piece of direct investigation was on pure impulse. It was a baking Sunday that late August and I remembered the local Spiritualist church held an afternoon service at which mediumship was demonstrated. Anne did not wish to go so I drove alone into town and then hovered outside the church, a little uneasy and embarrassed.

What if anyone I knew saw me going in?

The neighbourhood was depressing and the building nondescript. It was typical of my prejudices at that time that I didn't realise that a largely working class movement deriving from the mid-nineteenth century would hardly have had buildings to rival the great cathedrals of the Middle Ages or the solid, bourgeois foundations built by nonconformist industrialists in the Victorian period.

A plump youngish woman in a white dress stopped by me and gave her son money for the arcade machines round the corner.

Don't expect this every week.

He scooted off.

I've never been before. What's it like?

It's lovely. I go every week.

And in she went.

And so did I. A crumpled old boy stood at a table of hymn books and past copies of *Psychic News* and *Two Worlds*. I learned later that he was a gifted trance medium.

Shudder.

He gave me a hymn book and I sat in the back row, the seat nearest the exit, ready to slide out if I couldn't take it. The plump girl in white sat halfway down on the left. In the right hand front row an elderly woman in a wheelchair was being settled by her friend or carer. A raised platform ran along the back wall. It had a piano to the left, a door in the middle, and a dais on the right. At the piano was quite a pretty middle-aged woman with, and it delightfully confirmed all my prejudices, a look of absolute and soppy spirituality on her face. Would the medium come through the door when she started playing, or, a frivolous thought, pop up suddenly through a trap door like a pantomime devil?

The pianist's head wobbled and she struck up some vague all-purpose melody, glancing spaniel-like about her. We stood and sang a rather thin-blooded hymn. Then the door in the middle opened and a well built, medium sized woman (a medium sized medium) entered. Her rather grand manner seemed more appropriate to a bigger venue. She was followed by a tall, scholarly looking man with amiable features. He asked us to sit. He praised us for our loyalty in attending on such a lovely day and introduced the medium, from our sister church in the southern part of the county;

Those of you who have met her before know that we are in for a treat.

He stopped. Now was she going to perform? No, another hymn, which was sung with a little more beef behind it since one or two stragglers and late-comers had joined the congregation. We sat down again and waited. The medium from the south of the county, who was going to give us a treat, started to march up and down the platform. We got stars, we got flowers, we got spiritual evolution, we got self-esteem, motivation, all you need is love, we got God is colour blind, and a lot more. She finished with a flourish which seemed to invite applause. But none came. Instead, we were on our feet again, warbling another hymn as the pianist's head again moved insecurely on its foundations. We sat. If Ralph was watching this he'd be in hysterics by now.

We waited and waited in silence. Then she spoke.

I'm getting a photograph album. Has anyone been looking at photos recently? Can anyone take this and a large built gentleman who went over, suddenly, not long ago?

A hand shot up. It belonged to a middle-aged woman with thin, straight grey hair. She nodded.

He wants you to know that he's happy and that he's with you when you look at the snaps.

My cynicism expanded to fit the space available, and then some. She carried on.

I'm getting a man called Jack and a lady who passed over late in life after a blow to her arm.

Wow. My dad's name was Jack and my grandmother died in her late nineties after a fall. Up shot my hand. But unfortunately another hand had also gone up. It was the friend/carer with the lady in the wheelchair.

No, it's all right (I said) you go first.

I didn't really listen to her message. I was getting angry. The whole session just seemed to be an example of the stock mediumistic trick of fishing. Float a little generalised bait that could apply to many people and then reel them in one by one. Checking my irritation, I tuned in again to hear the medium getting a little irritated with the lady in the wheelchair. The poor woman was deaf and the medium had to relay the message to the friend/carer who shouted it in the invalid's ear.

Can you take this? Take what? That's what she said. Take this? What's she say? I've got a Vera here. She's got Vera. Who? You know who — VERA. Vera?

And so it went.
Then she turned to me.

I'd like to come again to the gentleman at the back. I am still getting the name Jack. It is on a father vibration and it is for you. He tells me he is very happy with what you have achieved in life. He is wishing you peace and happiness and is sending me pictures of the countryside.

She got the name right. I do live in the countryside. The common sense side of me said so what. But I was moved, annoyed that I was moved, and began to realise the seductive power of such performances. At the end of the service the medium came and stood by the old boy with the hymn books at the back and it appeared we were supposed to thank her as we went out. She stood very erect, imposing and theatrical. I just thought that she liked a captive audience and went home unimpressed.

I was glad Anne had not come, but I was determined to continue and realised that, though the woman I had seen might well have gifts and just had an off day, public demonstrations were probably too crude and showy. Only contact on an individual basis with a good medium would do. But how was I to go about this?

October

Much to my amazement, my youngest sister provided the key. She was an attractive, fit, slim blonde of about forty at the time of Ralph's death. She was my parent's last child and had been rather spoilt. I am the eldest of seven. The gap between us was, therefore, large and we did not meet very often. But she—who I had last seen years before at my Grandmother's ninetieth—had turned into a very interesting and sensitive woman. She was qualified in the practice of Reiki and only some time after Ralph's funeral, while searching through various spiritual/new age websites, did I discover that she was working with one of the UK's leading psychics and was heavily involved in the very area that I wished to investigate. I asked if she could arrange a sitting for us. He was very busy, she said. However, if I was patient, he would give us a private reading at some time, if we could get to his house in the South East.

I got one of his books from the library. He didn't look at all spooky, if the picture on the back cover was to be trusted. My sister said that he was a very unpretentious and straightforward man with none of the self-importance and self-dramatisation that such people sometimes had. Thank God, I thought, thinking of the medium in the local Spiritualist church.

She made most of the arrangements and we drove across country in early October 2002 to have a sitting with him. He had a large detached house on a pleasant estate. His wife met us at the door holding a conversation with her daughter about supper. This was all very normal and reassuring. She showed us the garden entrance to his office and where he was waiting for us. The first thing I noticed was the intensity of his blue eyes when we shook hands. A cliché but it was true. We sat down: Anne on a chair and I scrabbled around, eventually finding a footstool of some sort. The medium sat in an open-necked shirt and slacks facing us. The walls were lilac coloured – an unusual colour. The last time we had seen such a colour was on the walls of Ralph's bedroom as a child. There was a large bookcase on one wall full of spiritualist literature, and there were two desks behind him, each with an Apple Mac on them. The room displayed the general mix of clutter and order of any office working space. There was absolutely no sense of it being organised to induce a particular mood or manipulate sitters.

He said that he could guarantee nothing and then was quiet for a moment or two and started. He did not go into trance but talked quite normally as if relaying straightforwardly messages from someone on the other end of a telephone. He spoke quite quickly and made, in general, positive and specific statements. There was no hesitancy or fishing. We were obviously in a heightened and emotional state but we both felt a strong sense of communion with Ralph and relief that he was all right, whatever all right meant in this strange context. However, we were also aware of the susceptible condition we were in, and over white wine and fish at a nearby restaurant we carefully picked over and wrote down each individual statement that he had made. It was a pity that I did not tape record the session (as I did with all later ones except one where the tape player malfunctioned). I had not yet fully appreciated the importance of accurate and if possible verbatim records.

With this sitting, and all those in the future, I decided to pick out all the main statements made and to analyse them under the following headings: true, false, other (not possible to verify, for whatever reason), and predictive (might be true or false in the future). I go into the reasons for this approach in Part 2 when I discuss issues and problems to do with the objective assessment of information that mediums provide. There is a detailed table listing the results of all ten sittings over the years at Appendix 1.[1]

Sitting with medium 1 (male)
9.10.2002. Anne and Trevor present. South East.

There is a young man here	True
Died in an accident	True
He passed over very quickly	True
He was not in full clarity of mind	True
He had been drinking but was not much over the limit	True
He had made a mistake and he had paid the price	True
Parents not to worry re inquest. They won't be affected	Pred
He did suffer remorse but has come to terms with it	Other
Another person involved? Saw a windscreen shattering?	True
Car a write off	True
No pain. The body felt pain but he had left it.	
* He was jammy.*	Other

---

[1] All true statements can be verified either by documentary evidence and/or the memory of more than one person.

Sense of a mischievous and teasing personality	True
Very popular person	True
Had a good mind	True
Could have got more A's	True
Liked unusual animals	True
Neat but casual dresser and didn't like wearing ties	True
Liked music	True
And music at funeral was unusual	True
Had long fine hair	True
Some hair was taken from him	True
He was fond of travel	True
Spent time in Australia	True
Something soft in the coffin from childhood	True
Love of water sports	True
He'd stayed too long at home but it was changing	True
He had sorted his career	True
Mainly pressure from his mother	True
She was grieving a lot	True
Ralph was with her	Other
She had a love of gardens and plants	True
Talked to Ralph at the grave	True
She and Ralph had a very close relationship	True
A pair of shoes?	Other
He was sensitive about his right ear sticking out	True
He was doing a crap job	True
An imbecile could do it and an imbecile did	True
Had a sentimental, kind-hearted, romantic side	True
Has met lots of people this side. Finding out about them	Other
Keen to explore and find out	Other
Met his grandmother and Mrs Bennett	True
Old fashioned ladies. Ice cream and jelly	True
Upset about their houses. Thought they'd be there forever	True
A car park now there	True
Met Grandad Nelson	Other
A biggish man	True
Sense of humour	True
Met big, sharp-tongued, jowly woman	True

Name like a flower	True
Reference to bikes and her	True
She mentions a ring	True
He has spent time with her but not too much	True
Who had bad feet, bad legs?	Other
The name Peter	True
Comes back to house to see us	Other
Loved the kitchen – the granite tops	True
An older style kitchen	True
His bedroom as a child was lilac coloured like this office	True
It had a basin in it	True
Someone wearing a wig	True
Father liked France and its wines	True
Recently changed jobs	True
Doesn't like travel and should spend money on it	True
Ralph gave a wink (a code from childhood)	True
Singing song over grave? Big Rock Candy Mountain?	True
The 6th of July means something	True

The assessment of the sitting with medium 1

How were we to handle and make sense of this material spilling from the medium's lips? He spoke quickly and confidently and even when he raised a question, moved on without waiting for an answer. I am sure that by our body language and occasional comments he would have been reassured that he was making a positive impression, but that does not explain the number of accurate factual statements that he made.

The problem was how to assess the relative importance of these statements since not all of them were of the same degree of specificity. To put it heartlessly, some of the statements referring to Anne were what one would expect of any mother and child. Though others concerning her and me were more precise. Anne did sing the song Big Rock Candy Mountain over his grave and had also sung it to him in his early childhood. I can remember lecturing Ralph pompously about how I preferred the more subtle French wines to the blockbuster American ones. He used to tease me about going bald and claimed I was wearing a wig and the wink was a code between us from his childhood.

Underneath that wonderful exultant feeling, which we both wondered at and bathed in, at the sitting, and over the meal afterwards—that there was something in this, that he had survived—there was a nagging sense of the complexity of it all. I remember, as I started on my analysis of that first sitting, the energy draining out of me. I stared bleakly, rather hopelessly, out of my study window at the colourless sky and the great beech trees about to lose their leaves. What kind of statements would give us evidence of Ralph's continuing existence? It all seemed so bloodless, unreal, and pointless, and resolutely verbal, compared to him actually being here, back with us.

Still, I forced myself to persist with the exercise. I would expect there to be statements that were not in the public domain and, if known by others or written down, to have required huge, almost impossible efforts of ingenuity to acquire. I would also expect there to be sufficient flavour in the statements of the unique personality of the individual purporting to communicate. I would hope that the statements made were precise and unambiguous and could be confirmed objectively either by physical evidence or the testimony of people other than ourselves. But this was in an ideal world. Were there any mediums that good? However, I was encouraged by my discovery (as I started research on his biography) that these criteria, phrased in a more grandiloquent late-Victorian style, were virtually those that Myers had laid almost exactly a hundred years before (Hamilton, 2009: 175):

> 'First the need of definite facts, given in the messages, which were known to the departed and are not known to the automatist; and secondly, the need of detailed and characteristic utterances; a moral means of identification corresponding to the... individual complex of minute markings left by the impression of a prisoner's thumb.'

However, even though the statements made might seem very precise and relevant to us, maybe they were just the kinds of statements that a crafty and plausible medium would throw out based on his knowledge of people, their life situations, and the way they presented themselves to him? They did not seem to be but I made a mental resolve to look at this later in detail, and I discuss this in some depth in Part 2. I might need a more discriminating classification than just 'true or false'. But this would do for now.

All the comments about Ralph were accurate and were capable of confirmation by us and, more objectively, others. He had a mischievous and teasing personality. He was very bright and only at university did he start to realise his potential. He was neat but hated wearing ties. It was a gargantuan battle to get him to wear one at his degree award ceremony, and even then he refused to wear a jacket under his gown! He spent a considerable amount of time in Australia. He loved surfing and had surfed in North Devon. He was buried in his grandmother's shawl (*something soft in the coffin from childhood*). Eventually at 27 he decided to be a teacher and he got onto a PGCE course at the local university. I had helped him a lot with that, though his mother had probably been the more persistent agitator getting him to sort his life and career out. He had had some cannabis and ecstasy at the time of his death, and he was a little over the alcohol limit. Those statements were confirmed at the inquest, which did not affect us, in the sense that a distressing verdict of suicide was not delivered. His car crashed into a bus, so those facts were broadly accurate. The details about his boring administrative job were accurate, as was his concern over his right ear (verifiable from photographs) and his self-deprecating comments about himself. He was romantic and kind-hearted. Many friends testified to this.

When Anne was teaching she often left the boys with my grandmother and her friend from next door, Mrs Bennett. They did feed the boys up on things like jelly, ice cream, and cake. They were thoroughly spoilt. Grandad was a biggish man with a sense of humour. But his name was Jim not Nelson. Nelson, interestingly, was another relative who had passed on, and if one accepts the Spiritualistic hypothesis, it would be only natural for some confusion to occur in the eager rush to provide verifiable information. My grandmother and Mrs Bennett lived in their houses for three quarters of the twentieth century. They were rented and on their leaving the houses were sold to a developer and turned into flats. When I visited the area some years later I found that all of their gardens and, it appeared, the backs of the houses, had been turned into car parking spaces. I did not know this at the time. My wife recognised the description of her Aunt Ivy — the woman with a name like a flower — and she was wearing a ring which had been Ivy's. She was a rather talkative and tart individual, and the comment about spending some time with her *but not too much* seems a nice touch.

His fondness for our new kitchen and the kitchen surfaces was true, as was the description of the bedroom he occupied for many years, its unusual colour, and the fact there was a basin in it. The date of July 6th was particularly significant. That was the evening he went out with his friends which, in turn, led to his death on the 7th. He had very nearly decided to stay in and to ask his girlfriend round. But he changed his mind at the last minute. Had he stayed in on the 6th......?

We felt, making what allowances we could for our state of mind, that much of the above information was verifiable and almost impossible for the medium to have researched. There had been no news item on the crash except for a very short report in the local paper which gave very little detail. The report of the inquest was not available till a couple of months after the sitting.

To cap it all, at about this time we received a death grant, paid to us as Ralph's next of kin, by the government department he was working for at the time of his death. I, of course, immediately remembered the very first medium's statements about a burden to bear and receiving a lump sum. This was the department, incidentally, which had treated me with great kindness and courtesy when I had gone round to clear Ralph's desk.

The accuracy of the session gave us considerable material for reflection. Anne, I think, was happy at the result. It certainly helped her with grieving and she did not feel the same need for further research and continued validation that I did. I had to know. Were all sittings as good as that one? How could I work out whether I was being conned or not? So, passing the local Spiritualist church, shortly after this first reading, I noticed an advertisement for a visiting medium from the South East who was offering one to one consultations. I went in and booked one.

His style and approach were rather different from medium 1's but the reading was also interesting. He was a dapper, middle-aged man, of darkish complexion, with thick glasses. A neatly rolled umbrella lay on a chair. Unlike the first medium he had a tape and tape recorder to hand, so that I had the original words to examine later. Again, unlike the first medium (who appeared to find conventional Christian objections to Spiritualism irritating) he framed his reading in a broadly Christian context and he introduced it with a prayer. That suggested another thread for me to investigate later. Why were the Churches so hostile to Spiritualism and were there any individuals, in either camp, who were prepared to build bridges? One would have thought that they would be on the same side. I later realised how naïve this instinctive response of mine was.

Sitting with medium 2 (male)
15.10.2002. Trevor present. West Country.

Let us join together in a short prayer.

Then he paused for a moment and started the communication just like the first medium, without any sense of going into an altered state of consciousness, certainly not anything that could be remotely called a trance.

You have a research interest in this as well as personal	True
This is a period of change and adjustment	True
You have seen the best of things in the past	True
You are doing now what you have wanted to do for years	True
This is a long term, new challenge	True
Spirit is very pleased with this	Other
There is a lot of talk of writing, freelance writing	True
I see you alone a lot	True
You and your wife do separate things	True
Both happy with this arrangement	True
Your father is here. Very unusual personality	True
Communication between you better when older	True
When young you could almost have called him sir	True
Inwardly he liked people being a little afraid of him	True
Didn't harm you. You've been a disciplined person	True
He passed with chest, bronchial, breathing problems	True
He is interested in your writing and will help	Other
Elizabeth Roberts was your music teacher	True
You played the piano and loved Chopin	True
I see the Rupert Bear image	True
Your father took the Daily Express for the racing results	True
You have a close link to your mother	True
I haven't her here today	True
She has a very good intellect and you have respect for her	True
Your father sends a lot of love to her	Other
Your father liked centre stage. He would hold court or not at all	True
He is very comfortable with this method of communication	Other
I get the name Mary	True
I get the name George	True
The name Sheila	True
A young man here	True
Passed quickly in the prime of life	True
He suffered a strong blow to the head	True
Very creative and sensitive lad	True
Has communicated before	True
Your relationship not like you and your father's	True

You had a strong intellectual link	True
He was sensitive to others' feelings	True
Never caused you any problems	True
Around 26 years old from appearance	True
Thinner, a bit taller than you with broader shoulders	True
Nice hair, open face and smile	True
Very quick mind and picked up on things quickly	True
Sends love to David	True
Catapulted into the world of spirit	True
He laughs and shows me a tin of shoe polish/brushes	True
You didn't realise till after his death how many he attracted	True
The name Juliette	False
He loved monkeys and the Monkey House	True
Your wife has found grieving harder	True
She wouldn't necessarily accept this method	True

The assessment of the sitting with medium 2

His style was a little slower and a little more pompous than the first medium's. He obviously liked the authority of his position but he seemed both genuine and kindly. He was quite right about the general circumstances in my life. I had retired from full-time work in 2001 (with no regrets), though I had taken up different part-time employment in 2002. His general comment about my state of mind could, of course, be based on the kind of mindset one would expect from a fifty-nine year-old man coming for a reading.

More surprising was his sensing of the nature of the task and challenge that I was beginning to create for myself in retirement. The Myers biography took an enormous amount of time and energy over the next few years, particularly as I was combining it with a demanding (nominally!) three days a week work. I was often at my desk—alone—for long hours at a stretch and I was very lucky that Anne was a strong personality with her own independent interests and pursuits. And he was right, too, that Anne was less interested in mediumship than I was.

On other details: the character sketch of my father was extremely accurate. He had been a warrant officer in the army. He was meticulously neat and punctilious, had little small talk and was a disciplinarian. When we were children he was often uncomfortable to be around and we would escape from the room he was in at the first available moment. He followed the horses, and the back pages of the Daily Express were his regular breakfast reading. He had a good brain and, these days, would certainly have gone on to higher education. He was a heavy smoker and drinker and died at seventy of complications associated particularly with the smoking. My mother also was and is intellectually acute and all her seven children have a great respect for her. It was surprising (and seems to happen with a number of mediums) that there is uncertainty as to whether the personality they are sensing is alive or dead. The scope for fishing here is obvious. I did have a music teacher called Elizabeth (Richards not Roberts) and I have always had a love of Chopin, which I used to play a lot in my teens.

What was surprising was that the medium needed prompting to sense Ralph. I had asked—my only intervention—was there anyone else he could make contact with, a young man? One would, therefore, expect someone who was a skilled fraud to anticipate that if I asked for a young man, that person was quite likely to have been my son and to have died in an accident and been in his mid-twenties. So that was not impressive—he had been quite well cued. The points, however, about his intelligence, sensitivity, and creativity were all accurate, as was his interest in monkeys. He was spot on, too, about his appearance though one would probably expect sons to be taller and thinner than their fathers! The point about his popularity and attractiveness had also been mentioned by medium 1 and that alarmed me a little. Was that the kind of standard patter that mediums came out with when they encountered grieving parents? The shoe polish reference had particular resonance for me. On one occasion, annoyed at my sons' casual approach to their appearance and clothes (they were around nine and eleven I think), I set about properly instructing them in the correct way to thoroughly polish their shoes, as I had learned from my own father. Unfortunately I hadn't got my father's sergeant majorly authority and we all three collapsed laughing after they had made a few inept efforts to please me.

He clearly did not go into trance, and commented on his own performance as the session went on. He asked very few questions and gave a detailed character description of my father without any prompting at all from me. I asked him about frequency of sittings with a medium. He replied that it was a thoroughly natural but imperfect method and that a well balanced person should sit as often as they wished.

The sitting was a good one. However, I found the occasional throwing out of names irritating: George, David, Juliette, Mary, Sheila. I could put a personality to most of these names but so could virtually anybody. Sheila was my mother's Christian name and George my wife's father's second name, and so on. But it seemed a pretty pointless exercise.

2003

January to July

The impact of the original sitting remained with us and helped us through the gnawing pain of bereavement, as did, to some extent, the second sitting. But there were painful, practical things to cope with that constantly reminded us of our and Dan's loss. I had to sort out the legal matters to do with Ralph's death. I remember going to the registrar to prove probate and get the death certificate, and sitting outside her office staring at the little table in front of me, tapping aimlessly with a couple of pennies on the table top, confronted by the utter meaninglessness of it all. I also (though thankfully the insurance company dealt with the details) had to receive copies of correspondence about the claims for compensation that came in from the people who were on the bus that he had collided with (claims that came in at irregular intervals over a number of years and caused us searing pain). To us—no doubt unfairly—it seemed they were all out to make a quick buck from our son's death and our distress, using the no-win-no-fee system that had become so popular. In addition, I had to close his bank account and contact the Student Loans Company.

The inquest was an interminable time coming and we did not feel we could properly grieve in a settled way until it was over. The verdict was accidental death. Ralph had only been slightly over the limit from alcohol, but it was obviously the impact of the ecstasy and the cannabis combined with the alcohol that had affected his judgment.

One local paper excelled itself. The first story in July 2002 before the inquest had tried to create the picture of a teenage joy-rider who had crashed while his careless parents had been jet setting around the world. Ralph was 27 and we had been on a short break to Paris. The second story in the same paper after the inquest gave the impression that Ralph had been driving round the West Country out of his head and had crashed on his way home. In fact, he had not done any driving at all. He had left the car at his friend's house on the coast before a non-drinking driver took them to the various events.

The inquest took place at exactly the time David Blunkett announced an easing in the attitude towards the taking of cannabis. As a consequence of this we experienced two very unpleasant examples of the press trying to use our grief and our loss as a way of making copy. The first one was from another local paper. There trickled down the phone an oily pseudo-sympathetic voice:

Mr Hamilton? So sorry to hear about your recent tragic loss. In the light of the Home Secretary's blah blah blah, have you anything you'd like to say to him?

I have no comment. Not now, not ever.

Phone down.

A few days later. Ring at the door. Anne answered and immediately called up the stairs to me.

Darling, it's the ---

I went down. A tubby woman, rather crumpled, stood in the doorway, apologetic, slightly craven. She seemed to hint: I am no threat, I am only doing my job, please be nice to me. Again, there hung around her the same atmosphere of synthetic concern that I had detected in the earlier phone call from the journalist. She had her upper arms over her breasts and her hands covered her lower body. That was what gave her the pleading look. I realised she must have been trained to approach like that: part protection, part appeasement.

Mr Hamilton? I'm from the—

I have no comment. Not now, not ever.

I shut the door in her face.

As well as my research on Myers, I began to read round in the general literature and it struck me — could I become a medium? I had the potential, if the very first medium was to be believed. However, I quickly realised that this was unworkable. How could I ever convince myself, let alone other people, that I wasn't deceiving myself and subconsciously making things up, in such a personal matter? I was, however, vaguely aware of a process called electronic voice communication (the departed apparently communicating onto a running tape recorder against a background of radio white noise). See Part 2. This, though *a priori* absurd, even grotesque, attracted me since it seemed to provide an objective physical phenomenon that could be examined in detail.

So I solemnly followed the instructions that I had gathered from various sources and went to work. It appeared that the white noise between short wave radio stations was the best carrier for spirit voices. So I tuned to this. I had also heard that running water helped. I didn't, however, like the idea of keeping the tap in the washbasin of one room running while I recorded for an hour or so. But I tried and I tried, attempting to record at the same time every other evening, using earphones, not using earphones, raising and lowering the volume. There was hissing, there was the picking up of distant, etiolated sounds around the house, there was a low rumble, which was the tape mechanism, and there was, after a while, other noises.

Eventually, I began to pick up high, whispery traces of what appeared to be conversations. I felt like some frustrated MI5 or GCHQ eavesdropper whose equipment would never allow him to get close enough to the source. Also, I had to guard against the inevitable temptation of reading meaning into the hissing and jumbled sounds. Each time I started, I would ask Ralph to talk to me if he wanted to. Each time all I could clearly make out was my own voice, pompous and archly self-conscious. Each time, well-fuelled by wine, I would get down on my knees and listen to the tape, or sit at my desk with the earphones on, gazing out of the window at the shimmering silver birch, hoping against hope for something to come. But nothing ever did.

Sometimes my attitude reminded me of our friend in the village who had helped make Ralph's funeral so wonderful. At the time her hair was dyed red. Was she the red-headed woman referred to in the sitting before Ralph's death? She had worked so hard, so lovingly with Anne to find a community focus to celebrate his personality and remember his passing—the decorated coffin, the church given over to a celebration of his life and personality—but at times, rather unfairly, we sometimes felt we were just a topic in her Masters in Community Arts. I didn't want to feel that Ralph was just part of a project.

As time went on some of Ralph's friends dropped by and we learnt more about him—little bits dropped as glittering asides that Anne and I swooped upon like jackdaws. I didn't know that—did you? The first I didn't know was drugs. I didn't want to know. I had always been against cannabis and had been teased by Anne for it.

You went right through the sixties with your short back and sides and books and beer. You are an unreconstructed fifties man.

Ralph slyly kept quiet about all that. He drank conventionally heavily and partied, and then seemed to go for long periods without any activity of that sort. In our presence he just presented a slightly grumpy, sardonic, teasing personality, occasionally sour and withdrawn, and taking the parental home for granted. In other words, just like millions of other adult children. The parents are only fed certain things and usually in a way that the child knows will instantly play on parental guilt.

The second thing was his music. I didn't realise how good he was. He never pushed himself forward and I was instinctively conservative in these matters. The music of the last band he was in, which we played at his funeral, was a revelation to me, with its haunting, melancholic undertones, and its seamless changes of pace and mood, like a top athlete going up a gear. The band's record had been reviewed in the musical press and they had played on television.

And the third thing was love. I was amazed at the affection in which he was held by his peers. He was both the manic, impish clown and the person who listened, who talked things through.

He helped me sort myself out.

So said one shy, thin lad at his funeral. Two of his friends, for several years after, made long journeys on the anniversary of his death to visit his grave, and sometimes we would spot flowers there from we knew not whom, including one which sweetly had the note

Petal, we miss you.

As well as dealing with Ralph's death, Anne and I also had to come to terms with its impact on our relationship. It could have gone either way. Often bereaved couples break up. The death imposes too great a strain and brings to the surface fault lines and cracks which had been slowly developing anyway. Luckily that did not happen with us. However, in the heightened emotional state of bereavement, anything could erupt and it sometimes did.

In the spring of 2003 the village pub started to do regular fish and chip takeaway. This seemed to appeal to the stolid middle class English psyche in a way that more exotic offerings like Greek/Italian/Turkish/Hawaiian (in desperation) had not. We met nice people there (also ordering and collecting their takeaway), but having had a glass before we went and one there, if we were caught just as others were coming in, we would have a third. And it was always the third glass that caused trouble. Back in the kitchen we set to the fish and chips and the argument began. Anne has a tendency instinctively to the collective left and I (who would dearly like to pretend to an Olympian impartiality) have a gut reaction in favour of order and authority until convinced otherwise. So I said, without emphasis, but merely en passant of something she said

That's a bit like the phrase you trotted out the other day.

I did not mean anything by it but she erupted.

That's typically dismissive of you, typical Oxford, in a minute you'll talk about my knee-jerk left wing reactions.

So, of course, nettled, and thinking myself unfairly attacked, I did.

After a little while we both backed off and resumed picking off the chips and, opening out the clean, flavoursome cod inside the deep fried batter, thinking about the things that lay behind the spat. I knew some—Anne went to Cardiff University. She was intuitive, warm-hearted, engaging. I was Oxford, pontifical, cerebral. She was annoyed at my vanity and pomposity while I sometimes thought, although I envied her insight into contemporary culture, that some of the fashionable gurus she quoted were specious. There were other factors too. In the early 1980s when I was doing my most miserable job, 1st Deputy Head in a comprehensive school, she was a lecturer in a tertiary college in the city, meeting a wide variety of stimulating and interesting people in a lively and raffish intellectual environment. I was frankly jealous of that. I would come back dog-tired in the evening having spent my day disciplining bored adolescents, dealing with difficult colleagues, juggling competing demands (I once logged, as an experiment, nearly one hundred matters in the first hour of the school day that I was expected to deal with), interceding between the Head and the staff, chasing smokers, investigating thefts, doing the timetable, preparing the material for inspection, and so forth, only to hear her at dinner talking amusingly of postmodernism (whatever that was) and the sexual entanglements of her colleagues. We were on different planets, and the memory of those ghastly years still stayed with me. A further tension was that I did not fully appreciate at the time the problems she was going through, as a married woman returning to the workplace, and the many pressures that placed on her. And above all there was the mutual guilt, that had we organised our lives better maybe we could have avoided this appalling tragedy.

But that evening, after we had calmed down, she startled me with another comment.

I know Ralph deeply loved me as child to mother before adolescence, and he moved away from me as he got older, pushing me off, but you must feel terribly lonely now. He understood you, appreciated your mind, your way of thinking, because it was his way too. And you would have grown closer together in this as he got older.

I remembered, at the same table, shortly before he died, he gave a vivid analysis of the management weaknesses of the government department in which he was working and I praised him enthusiastically for it. He was prone to making self-deprecating remarks about himself but he was really very able. He had good analytical skills, even though in his current job he had no opportunity to use them, and even needed convincing that they were valuable.

Anne and I understood what each of us had lost by his death and we used that understanding to bring us closer together. We saw how silly and superficial (though we still enjoyed giving each other a good verbal biffing) our vanities were compared to our love for each other, him, and his brother. We would work through this together.

Anne was particularly supportive to me with regard to one unexpected consequence of Ralph's death. I began, for the first time in my life, to get a sense of paranoia, that I was suspect in some way and that people were out to get me. Anne dismissed this and said that what really lay behind it was loss of control. Ralph's death was the first significant occasion when something really important had happened to me in my married life that was not soluble by working harder or trying to behave better. My professional life had been tempestuous and full of challenges, particularly in its later period. But I had risen to those challenges and overcome them. Anne and I had had a period of real difficulty in our married life, and I recollected sliding down the wall halfway up the staircase one August in the 1990s, drunk and hugely melancholy, watching the startlingly bright moonlight flood in through the unclosed curtains, thinking that I was unhappier than I had ever been in my life, but that I was going to get through it. I remember, too, my determination (and Anne's) not to let Ralph or Dan sink (both of us feeling that we had not been sufficiently involved with them in their teens), and how we supported and cajoled them through university. And they achieved 2:1s, after, both of them, rickety and aimless periods in their early twenties. We did not lose them. They did not sink. Anne and I did not part. The bad guys did not win at work. And yet this I could not sort and it opened a window for me onto a world of bleak uncertainty where great effort, good intentions, a sense of justice, meant nothing in the face of blind circumstance.

This incipient paranoia was also fed by the attitude of a number of friends, socially and at work, to my statements that I was both researching mediumship in connection with Ralph's death and, more widely, working on the history of psychical research. Some were sympathetic and curious, but others gave the impression that I was unbalanced by grief.

The concerned look in the college librarian's eye when she saw the titles of the two PhD theses that had arrived for me—the fact that they were kosher theses from the British Library meant nothing. What was important was that they both had the word 'Spiritualism' in their titles. I vividly remember the gentle frisson from some colleagues when at a staff development session I unwisely used some of my work from the web on Spiritualism as a demonstration of the virtues of the online library that I had discovered.

Almost the only respectable way to approach the subject seemed to be to debunk it or warn people against the imposters who lurked in its dark and sinister woods, to see it as a psychological issue (what sorts of people believe in the supernatural and why), as part of the cults problem, or as an amusing cultural studies way into intellectual and social history. I longed to be able to discuss the subject—as well as my own personal quest—with people who had open minds, who were well read in the field and who, like me, felt that it was logically, practically, and blindingly obviously the most important single issue that there was. Did we survive bodily death, and if so what did this tell us about the nature of reality, and, fundamentally important, how we should live? But such individuals were few and far between.

August to December 2003

One thing strongly sustained me—the frequent positive dreams that I had about Ralph. On one occasion we sat talking at the table as he explained his philosophy of life and then did joyous cartwheels round our new kitchen which he liked so much. Dan, too, sometimes had such dreams, and on the Monday of August bank holiday weekend rang and told us one. It was as if Ralph had made the transition and we weren't to worry. Anne, sadly, did not have such dreams, and it was partly in the hope of further contact for her that we arranged to see a medium in the Midlands, again one whom my sister Carolyn had recommended.

We combined the visit with three days at a comfortable hotel in Dovedale where we also decided to have dinner with a couple of Anne's friends, whom I had not yet met. The setting was splendid, the hotel architecture was a little bland but it was circled by impressive limestone hills. On the second day, after a look at Buxton and its beautifully restored Opera House, we drove to the medium's home. We rang the bell and he, tall, amiable, slightly earnest, let us in. We had a good cup of coffee with him and his partner. This pleased Anne who was an expert in good and bad cups of coffee. I have lost count of the number of times a meal out has had a bad coffee denouement.

After this he positioned his chair in the corner between the chimney and the wall to help the energy build up, he said. It appeared that his partner was to act as the chairperson and record the session on the computer. We were a little uneasy at this. We had not expected a mistress of ceremonies. He discussed with us whether he would go into trance or his usual direct intuitive communication, and then said he would like to try trance as he was developing it. His partner then explained the difference between the two methods and how they related to the different types of brain rhythms from alpha to theta. We sat a long time waiting for him (he had taken his shoes off — why, we didn't know). Anne and I gave each other slightly puzzled looks but eventually he started to speak. His voice was quite normal in pace and tone and there seemed to be no evidence of trance.

Afterwards we took them for a meal and they talked about themselves and their future plans. Anne and I later wondered if there was some tension between them that sprang from their different approaches. He seemed to have a genuine if spasmodic gift and she was more managerial and analytical. She said that she did not work as a medium but as a natural law philosopher. Her job was to explain to people the way things were: the spiritual laws of the universe like Karma, etc. It would have been easy for the sniffy intellectual in me to wonder what Isaiah Berlin or A.J. Ayer would say about that—let alone Kant or Wittgenstein—but she had a point. Spiritualism should not just be about spooky manifestations. There needed to be a philosophy and a morality, as I later found there was, though the evidence from the paper, *Psychic News* that I briefly subscribed to was that the movement seemed to suffer from a distressing amount of superstition and infighting and not much calm thinking.

The sitting with medium 3 (male)
27.8.2003. Anne and Trevor present. Midlands.

Reference to a lot of R initials	*True*
The name Francis	*True*
The mother figure stroked his hair after he died	*True*
He had a friendship link with Glasgow	*True*
Elderly gentleman	*True*
Bald-ish. Glasses.	*True*
Teeth more out than in	*True*
Died of bronchial problems	*True*
The name Roger	*True*
The young man is doing star jumps	*True*
He's saying don't forget my eyes	*True*
References to white lilies at his feet after he died	*True*
Calling out mum to let you know he's been around	*Other*
There is a particular smell you've been smelling	*True*
Somebody has been holding an item of his clothing recently	*True*
He had a high-sided pair of trainers stored	*True*
In the bottom of a cupboard on left hand side of his room	*True*
He is holding his wrists up. Possible suicide?	*Other*
Last time you saw him was in the kitchen	*True*
He flicked his hair in a jaunty manner	*True*
Told you (Anne) not to worry	*True*
He was excited and in a bit of a hurry	*True*
He's making a reference to the lights, the bloody lights	*True*
(To Trevor) Take your time over trying to communicate	*True*
You've been getting snippets	*Other*
Three black bags of his clothes should go to charity	*Other*

He's referring to his candle	True
One of you is painting	True
He's painting a smiling bear to say pleased you are painting	Other
Picture of you (Trevor) agitated at a table	True
Tapping on it with a penny, in the registry	True
Waiting for a death certificate	True
Why the reference to two way radios?	True
Don't give up. Just listen for one word – father.	Pred
Reference to May 16th holiday	False
He is becoming a healer/skin diseases	Other
The father figure is singing that he has his sisters with him	True
Blondie. Can you place a Debbie or a Harry?	False
One of you is dreaming of him and remembering these dreams	True
I have to say three roses	True
He mentioned a leather jacket	True
He is showing me orange flowers – marigolds? – in the garden	True
Someone named John	True

The assessment of the sitting with medium 3

In the context of our relationship with Ralph, we could personalise and make sense of a number of the things that the medium said, but the reading did not have the urgency, directness, and conviction and specificity of the first one. We believed he was genuine but that he had not been on top form. This was confirmed by my sister when she read the transcript. She said he was known as one of the best young mediums in the Midlands and the North and this was not one of his best performances.

However, I found him very open and prepared to discuss with us what he was seeing and how it was possible to misinterpret the images. For example, when he had suggested possible suicide, he had based this on the image of the young man holding up his wrists with the watch on them. It could well have been the watch that was most important. In fact, Ralph was inordinately proud of a splendid watch that his girlfriend at university had given him.

He did pick up on my misery at the Registrar's proving probate, on Ralph's fondness for skateboarding (if one stretches the references to star jumps), on his wearing my leather jacket, on his high-sided trainers, on our smelling cigarette ash (if one reads this in), on the lilies placed at the coffin, on my dreaming of him, on his friendship with Glasgow musicians, and on a number of other details of varying specificity.

We had mixed feelings as we discussed the session, but our partial disappointment was alleviated by our meeting with Anne's friends. I had never met them before and was delighted by their openness to the paranormal (one of them was in fact an experienced Reiki healer), and we had a lively and alcoholic discussion of all things spiritual and anomalous after dinner in the hotel bar, mystifying, if not mildly alarming, a number of the business customers or conference attendees.[2]

A little dissatisfied with this session, I decided to have another sitting with the visiting medium who came fairly regularly to the local Spiritualist church (medium 2). Anne had found his tone slightly pompous when she listened to the recording and, not wanting to have the excellent first sitting further compromised, let me go alone.

Sitting with medium 4 (male)
16.9.2003. Trevor present. West Country.

He did not appear to recognise me, though at the end he said that he had a vague feeling that we had had a sitting before. I put that in for what it is worth. It certainly weakens the evidential aspect depending on his ability to retain the individual

---

[2] Over the coming years the Reiki healer appeared occasionally to receive messages from Ralph. On one occasion I had been shopping for socks (which I did not buy). That lunch-time I sat in glorious sunshine with a pint and mentally said to Ralph, 'Come on, for your mother, let's have some more evidence'. Shortly after this, Anne received a phone call from her friend saying, 'I have to tell Trevor to buy the big socks'.

details of readings for a variety of individuals in a range of places and conditions and circumstances. In his preamble he stated that it was all an experiment and that he should be judged purely on results. He didn't like vague generalities. Then he made a brief prayer and started.

Things are changing around you	True
You are coping with events outside your control	True
Look to the future	Other
Your past abilities will help you deal with things	True
Your finances will be OK	Pred
I get the name Peter	True
A relative comes	
Your father	True
A private undemonstrative man	True
He went quickly around the age of 70	True
Sometimes he surprised you with what he said	True
Fastidious and neat and meticulous	True
Right behind you in your endeavours	Other
A versatile man	True
Your mother is still here	True
Father sends love	Other
Lot to be admired about your mother	True
Much more a people person than your father	True
Interested in what is going on	True
Lot of respect for her	True
Sometimes too independent for her own good	True
Needs help unobtrusively	True
Good health	True
She made a good adjustment to her husband's death	True
Better than he would have done	True
I see you alone a lot	True
You and your wife are used to doing separate things	True
You have it as you like	True
There is a Mary in spirit	True
Mother's mother comes	True
Nice skin and complexion	True
Neither she nor your mother looked their age	True

An active grandmother	True
Helped bring you up: a second mother	True
I get your grandfather not so strongly: carpentry/making things	True
I'm getting the name Jack	True
Young man who passed as result of accident. An impact	True
Not old 18/20	False
Has a boyish face. Very lively, very eager	True
Lots of happy memories	True
Was cheeky	True
Open nature. No complications	True
You didn't realise how popular he was till you saw the numbers at the funeral	True
Had a way with females	True
A complicated love life	True
He died just as things were starting to take off	True
Dad, I went doing what I wanted to do	Other
Speed played a part and human error	True
Very nice personality	True
Concerned about how your wife was coping	Other
The name Margaret	True
Vivacious infectious laugh	True
Passed without pain and quickly	True
Adjusted very well	Other
I get a picture from him of you putting pennies into a piggy bank	False
The names Mark and Chris	True
The name John	True

The assessment of the sitting with medium 4

Much of the sitting repeated the material of the previous contact with him. This could be interpreted in several different ways. He might just have remembered our previous encounter. He could have been getting the same broadly accurate information from the spirit world. Or he could have been playing the same standard cold reading routine that he would trot out for people of my age and type. However, two new features were added which were worth considering. Ralph had had a rather complicated love life and was attractive to women. Also, the picture of my grandmother, putting in an appearance for the first time, was quite accurate. My mother had seven children, and my grandmother, who was strongly maternal and who had lost a male child just after his birth, had helped bring the children up, particularly when my father went on army tours of duty abroad. My father's Christian name was given as was his mother's, which was Margaret.

2004

Friends who had suffered bereavements told us that it would take up to two years for the pain to become bearable. They were both right and wrong. Wrong in that it never went away. It was always a monster, easily aroused, just under the surface. But right in the sense that one learnt to cope, though not to completely control it. In such a state around the New Year I tried to review things so far and to see where all this was taking me.

I now had transcripts from four readings, an eclectic mix of additional apparently paranormal phenomena of varying power and authenticity, and also a substantial collection of texts on the paranormal that I had enthusiastically collected and, more importantly, largely read. It was essential, firstly, to keep grounded, and I was very grateful for my continuing professional work. Secondly, I needed to evaluate the experiences more systematically and started to think about the best way to analyse the material. I also wanted to try to put together some coherent, if highly provisional, explanation for the phenomena. If there was something in it all (vacuous phrase), what did that actually mean for us here and now? I really could see no point to all this unless it had an impact on our lives here, not necessarily in grand Mother Teresa gestures, I hadn't got that in me, but in some incremental improvement, a kind of spiritual Fabianism perhaps?

Also, on that New Year's Day in 2004, the hangover fading and the familiar rituals over, I just sat at the computer and wondered how well did I really know Ralph, how much could I remember about him? Would it all fade? Pre-adolescence he had been a delightful child—warm, open, hugely energetic and enthusiastic. I have a vivid image of him playing all day and into the night at Dungeons and Dragons with his brother Daniel and friends, haring round the large garden, questing, adventuring, and slaying the foe. And, I have another image of him at the swimming baths, doing the backstroke, his little face pale and taut with determination as he tried to keep up with the bigger boys in the swimming tests. With adolescence he became darker, withdrew from his intimacy with his mother, as I have mentioned. His relationship with me tended to be the grunting and the jokey—perhaps as with many Dads—though occasionally I would get the odd serious question which showed he was thinking.

He was taller than me (around 5'11") and just taller than his mother. They used to square up to each other at the mirror and ask me to arbitrate. Yet he was always complaining how small he was—his brother was 6'3". He was one of those people who had the capacity to look ugly and then on other occasions handsome, radiant, and engaging. He was particularly sensitive about his right ear sticking out and tried to disguise it in photographs and by wearing a soft, floppy hat. He loved monkeys and would visit zoos and monkey houses, had a gorilla in his car, and often made monkey-like faces and gestures round the house if in a good mood. Pictures of him as a child were lovely. He seemed to have a glow about him. He could be charming and was popular with women. Daniel always used to send him in first to make friends with girls when they were children. He had a sentimental and romantic side to him and was fundamentally a good person. Yet the break-up of his relationship at university, shortly before his finals, had led to a sometimes Shakespearean bitterness about the nature and motives of women, and we were very grateful to his last girlfriend for helping him to come through that dark time.

He was a reader and had a good sense of the strengths and weaknesses of argument and evidence. Yet, he undervalued himself, and was haunted by the idea that his degree was not relevant and practical enough. His degree was in politics. It really annoyed him that, in the West Country, the only job he could get was a crap telesales-type job (as he put it) or manual jobs like watering hanging baskets of flowers (which he did for a while, kept fully employed by the competitive floral rivalries of the local towns and villages). Only gradually did he come round to the idea that teaching — for which he would have displayed a considerable gift in the right environment — was an honourable and appropriate vehicle for his talents. I could see from his early adolescence where his strengths lay, but he fought shy, naturally, of anything that linked to me and teaching (in which I was for part of my career).

March to July

Anne's mother died in March 2004. She was 92, in a nursing home, and Anne was with her at the end. Her mother was in some distress and Anne was annoyed that the doctor had not arrived to give her a sedative — part of the nanny state that a competent nurse could not do it. Her mother was rather noisy. She shouted

Help me, help me

She asked Anne if she was dying. Anne said she was and that she would see her husband soon. Her mother clapped her hands and said

Goodie

She also kept looking into one corner — three or four times — as if she could see someone. But Anne could see nothing. On the night of her mother's death Anne told me that she was twice patted gently on the back in a comforting way — once upper back and once lower back—by someone or something. She was sure she did not imagine it. Yet, discussing this at a later date, she was not so sure. About this time we received a message from our friend the Reiki healer (she also had sporadic mediumistic gifts) whom we had met at Dovedale, who said that Hilda was with Ralph. It was a pity she did not pass this to us immediately but she said that she did not wish to check in case it was wrong. Anne then decided to have a sitting with the visiting medium I had sat with twice and who was back at the local Spiritualist church. He appeared to make contact with her mother who reassured Anne that she had done everything possible for her in her last years, which was what Anne was glad to hear, but the sitting petered out. The message was what she wanted to hear but part of me, cynically, thought it was just the kind of generalised waffle that one would expect from a fraud or someone without genuine gifts, or in this case, when the contact was weak and intermittent. Granted that he was genuine, it raised the question of timing of first contact. Was it too early? I had read in the Spiritualist literature that two months should elapse before contact should be attempted. On the other hand, there are a number of examples of impressive communication apparently being made almost immediately after death.

And I was not getting very far with my exploration of electronic voice phenomena. I would remove my earphones from their snappy little red container, the same colour as my childhood dinky toy cars, and I still got a frisson of pleasure whenever I saw the colour. But that was the only satisfying part of the whole process. So I gave up. However, my dreams about Ralph continued, as did the remarkable effects of the landing lights. Shortly after my decision to stop listening for electronic voices from the beyond, Dan and his girlfriend came to visit. One evening they went to a party and came back about 2.00 a.m. After they switched off the landing light, it flashed very vividly, great streaks of yellow-white light across the landing, with a vigour I had not seen before. I heard them exclaim and saw the lights myself as I opened our bedroom door.

It was a strange period. On the one hand I felt Ralph with me all the time: not the strong, almost overwhelming, sense of his presence as Anne had sometimes after his death. It was more like a tender background music. And the dreams continued. One dream was particularly vivid and moving. I had it very early on the morning (May 5th 2004) that we were to receive and have installed the dark marble headstone at his grave. I was sitting in a chair and Ralph was giving me a hug. Yet, on the other hand the electronic voice phenomena had proved a miserable failure, and Anne's sitting with a medium had been very mixed. So, we decided to try again, and found a local one whom someone had recommended to me. She lived in a small, slightly cute village about an hour's drive from our home.

Sitting with medium 5 (female)
22.7.2004. Anne and Trevor present. West Country.

A child of yours came in with you	Other
Not sure yet whether male or female	Other
Sudden death	True
No chance to say goodbye	True
A soul full of fun and laughter	True
I've got my music here	True
Nice hair	True
Parents really need answers	True
Gives a red rose with love	Other
A little naïve but not stupid	True
A strong sense of adventure and discovery	True
He was strong minded	True
He liked to mimic	True
Very clever	True
Had a bright future	True
Kissed his mother on head	Other
Not imagination	Other
He has called out to her	Other

Part 1: Experiences

A developed spirit	*Other*
Has come from a high place	*Other*
He has a brother in spirit	*Other*
Who decided not to come	*Other*
Get a strong feeling of travel with him	*True*
Looking at father (who doesn't like travel)	*True*
Very strong sense of humour	*True*
Throwing the initials R and J at me	*True*
Talking about a small piece in a newspaper	*True*
Also referring to something on his wrists	
He is handing me a watch	*True*
The name Tom	*True*
A hug for his father	*Other*
Didn't show how much I felt about you both	*True*
A soft hat of his	*True*
More often on floor than not	*True*
Lot of father's family here	*True*
A friend aunt who used to play the piano	*True*
A man called Albert	*True*
A grandfather who is very special	*Other*
Wears a military uniform	
And still telling us what to do	*True*
A grandmother	*True*
A great grandmother	*True*
The name John	*True*
Trouble about him	*True*
A tinny vehicle	*True*
He really loved the water and to go under it	*True*
He did not live with a lot of fears	*True*
Not easily swayed by other people	*True*
He had a characteristic smile and frown	*True*
He loved his bike as a kid	*True*
And his old Xmas annuals	*True*
My mum and dad are my friends	
Always were	*True*
Just getting his life together	*True*
Thought he had it cracked at last	*True*

Proud of his father and the way he bore himself	True
Carried himself in what he did in the way an officer would	True
You set good standards	True
Yet you both gave him a breathing space to sort himself out	True
He was good at education and there was more to come	True
A problem with his lower back	
Twisted it	True
There is a big garden and a seat where he is	Other
With the grandmother with the cough	True
She lost a lot of height	True
He was at her deathbed	Other
He has put a cup of tea by her	Other
They laugh a lot	Other
She has perfumed roses round her	Other
She was very good with her hands	True
He has a lot of books round him	Other
He has unusual things around him	Other
He needed healing after death	Other
Went to a blue place	Other
He kept me waiting but he is a lovely soul	Other
Not a do-gooder but came from a high place	Other
And affected the lives of others	True
He was on a different route home	
Because it was less used	True
You will get your book published	Pred

The assessment of the session with medium 5

One of the interesting things in this session was her failure to identify the sex of the communicator till relatively late in the sitting. Whether this was a factor in favour of her authenticity or otherwise is difficult to say. There were a large numbers of phrases that would seem standard in these kinds of settings which had to be discounted as evidence, even if in emotional terms they made sense to us. The two most consistent communicators through all the sittings were Ralph and my father, Jack, so it is interesting that the initials she got were R and J. There were a number of accurate statements that seemed persuasive. Anne was a little startled, later, by the reference to the brother who did not come. Some time after the birth of Dan she thought she was pregnant again and a little while later had a particularly heavy discharge. Was it just too bizarre to try to link these two items? And later, in the sitting with medium 7, there was a reference to a child who had decided not to be born. Was this another stock verbal trick in the Spiritualist repertoire to make the sitters even more vulnerable and receptive?

Nevertheless, our overall impression concerning the medium was of someone genuinely trying to feel her way through to the truth in what would always be difficult conditions. But one thing we found difficult to accept was the language of angels, lovely souls, and Ralph coming from a very high place. He had considerable gifts of sympathy and sensitivity and he was lively, humorous, and charming with his friends, though more masked with us, but the highly spiced spiritual language of the medium was not to our taste, even though we were moved by the reading and found much in it that was accurate.

She spoke clearly but very slowly as if she was concentrating hard to pick up a faint and fluctuating signal. She seemed to jump from image to image with no clear linear narrative. There were long pauses as she waited for the next image or sound or impression to emerge. It was as if she was trying to get a particular radio station and kept slipping off it. She did not fish by asking questions, but sat patiently till she made contact again. She spent more time on the nature of the afterlife than the other mediums, describing it as a very pleasant world of thought where people created their own environments and a world in which love and a code of ethics were predominant. This view of the afterlife was common in the literature, but for me the focus was on evidence for survival and at that stage I discounted anything of a broader, metaphysical nature.

2005

The year 2005 was a quiet year, mostly one of consolidation and preparation before the major primary research for the Myers book took place. I was not yet in a position to travel to work on archival sources as the demands of my nominally part-time job at the college were beginning to irritate and grate on me, and I almost found myself back in the old mindset and grind of being a full-time employee. However, I stuck it out and did as much background reading as I could. As I dug more deeply into the secondary literature—the *Journal and Proceedings of the Society for Psychical Research* and the great publications associated with it, *Phantasms of the Living* (1886) and Myers' posthumous masterpiece, *Human Personality and Its Survival of Bodily Death* (1903)—I began increasingly, in conjunction with the readings I had had, to allow myself to think that all this might possibly be true.

However, such feelings/semi-convictions, call them what you will, were fragile. And the terrorist events of 7/7/2005 plunged us right back into the original despair of 2002, but thankfully only briefly. That that ghastly event should have taken place on the third anniversary of Ralph's death, and that Dan, whom we were unable to contact for many hours, might have been killed by one of the bombs, just seemed a foul and ironic cruelty too far.

2006

I decided to completely retire this year and to concentrate on the research into mediums and on Myers. Gradually Anne and I evolved a pattern. I would go up to London to visit libraries and sit with mediums, and we would stay in a quiet hotel near the British Museum, convenient for Anne to visit museums and galleries and for me to walk (I liked walking around London) to three organisations: the Society for Psychical Research, the College of Psychic Studies, and the Spiritualist Association of Great Britain. Anne really didn't feel the need for further sittings and so I went alone, partly for contact with Ralph and partly for research purposes.

I gradually got to know the area well and came to realise how much of the early exploration of the Spiritualist movement happened in the Great Russell St area, and how central and well placed and well connected were the early members of the SPR—Frederic Myers and Edmund Gurney in Moon St and Clarges St respectively, the Albemarle Club nearby, where they took their wives (almost the only club where women were welcome), their visits to the future prime minister Arthur Balfour in Carlton Gardens where séances were held, and not all that far from there, 2 Richmond Terrace, where Myers' mother-in-law, the formidable and wealthy Gertrude Tennant, held court, with Gladstone just a couple of doors down.

We were in London in April 2006 and I decided to have a sitting with one of the well-known mediums of the old school. She was based at the College of Psychic Studies and I selected her because I found many of the descriptions of the other sensitives on the website frankly rather off-putting. I did not want to contact my spirit guides, get life advice, release the inner me, open my chakras, do automatic writing or paint spirit portraits, I just wanted a good old-fashioned no nonsense sitting designed to provide evidence for survival. The old school would do for me. When I sat with her she had a streaming cold so that the tissues on the table, which were thoughtfully provided for tearful and moved sitters, served, in her case, a dual purpose. She, too, did not appear to go into an altered state of consciousness, but just paused for a moment or two, then began.

Sitting with medium 6 (female)
4.4.2006. Trevor present. London.

There is a lady here. On a mother link	True
She is a grandmother	True
Not very tall	True
She spent quite a lot of time with you	True
Passed over in her late seventies	False
Problems with her heart	

Breathing problems,	
Pleurisy?	True
Your mother's health not too good at moment	Other
Has been worrying a lot	Other
A leg problem	True
Your father comes	True
Passed quickly around seventy	True
Wearing casual clothes	False
About your height	True
Didn't see eye to eye when younger	True
But bond grew stronger with age	True
You are more like your mother's side of the family	True
Got a lady, a sister link with your mother	False
You've had a difficult patch recently	True
Don't look back	Other
A young man here. Your son.	True
Blue shirt with sleeves rolled up	True
A little taller than you	True
Slender	True
Brown hair	True
You were bitter and angry about his passing	True
Better over here than an invalid with you	
Says your father	Other
He's doing all right	Other
Talked about pain in head and not being able to breathe	True
Blames himself for the passing	True
Knows he disappointed you re studies	True
Was confused and depressed but was beginning to sort things	True
You and he had a strong bond	True
Things could be up and down, however	True
He had a job but not a real career	True
He said he pushed a photograph of himself over recently	Other
He laughed that you wouldn't let him have a motorbike	True
Yet here he was over here	
He loved music and was trying to be a musician	True
Had reasonable success	True
He liked watching sport but not playing it	True

He had an old head injury which left a scar	*False*
Dave's all right	*True*
The name Steve	*True*
Showing me a blue car	*True*
Then a red car	*True*
Accident with this one	*True*
Quite a restless person as if he wants to be elsewhere	*True*
The name Ben or Beth	*True*
The name James	*True*
Has seen James	*Other*
The name Mark	*True*
Worries about his mother	*Other*
Guilt over the strain put on her	*Other*
The name Simon	*True*
Good that you are retiring but you need to keep busy	*True*
The name Chris	*True*
He was a bit cynical about religion, like you sometimes	*True*
He talks of a grandmother over here	
He knew her more than the other	*True*
He talked of going for an interview	*True*
More interested in it than what he was doing	*True*
There was a trip planned at the time of his passing	*True*
He liked travel and had spent time in Australia	*True*
He says Jonathan will be all right	*True*
Mentions the name William	*True*
Also George on a mother link	*True*
Also May or Mary	*True*
Father takes me over the border to Scotland	*True*
His mother has seen him since he passed	*True*
He was with her recently when she looked at cards	
Connected with him	*Other*
He used to tease her	*True*
Has a sister or sister-in-law upset your wife recently?	*True*
Don't be upset	*Other*
Your wife needs a holiday	*Other*
He spends time with his mother's mother	*Other*
Sees her as a strong woman	*Other*

Help Andrew   *True*

The assessment of the sitting with medium 6

Like medium 5 (who was also female) she took her time in her delivery. There were a number of longish pauses and then little spurts of activity. She quite often made comments like *I'll ask* or *what's that* or *we'll find out,* which created quite a strong — though totally non-evidential — impression of contact with someone. I was already beginning to notice a difference in mediumistic style between male and female and wondered whether this would be replicated in any further sessions I had. Mediums 1 and 2/4 had more self-confident deliveries, while the two female mediums seemed more intuitive and hesitant.

She was broadly accurate with a large number of relatively general statements, but there were none of the highly specific statements of medium 1 or 2. The family was originally Scots/Irish but *over the border* could mean anything. Ralph and my father again appeared, as did my grandmother. The point about not letting him have a motorbike was accurate as, in a grim way, was the characteristic remark of my 'father', *better over here than an invalid with you*. She also picked up on the fact that Ralph had spent time in Australia and was planning a trip at the time of his death, as had medium 1, and the nature of his passing, as did the other mediums. His character and personality were depicted accurately as was his interest in music. I had had an accident in a red car shortly before the sitting but there was no mention of who had had the accident. Ralph had driven, at one period, a grey/blue car. There was the usual irritating spraying of names. I/we could identify all of them, but so could many other sitters.

The image of my father in casual clothes was interesting. In life he was a formal dresser. He was smart and pretty well all the mediums mentioned this attribute in some form or another. I can only really remember seeing him in a very casual cardigan on one occasion and this rather startled me.

Yet Anne, in commenting on this sitting, said that she recollected him towards the end of his life beginning to wear such an item.

June 2006

I decided to attend a conference on the development of mediumship. I did not want to become a medium myself but at least it would give me some insight into the processes (which would help with the judgment of evidence), and it would reduce my sense of isolation and give me a chance to talk to people with shared interests.

So, I booked in to attend a conference at one of the Spiritualist churches in the region — a four-day event on the exploration of the amazing power of spirit led by two people whose names seemed to have come straight from a monologue by Alan Bennett. All my 'nothing worthwhile exists north of Guildford' snobbery came to the fore. It was shameful and totally unfounded. But it was there. They were splendid people, but the northern stream of spiritualism seems to be very strongly working class and it is sometimes flavoured with a kind of cosy, unpretentious, faintly saucy humour of the Donald McGill seaside postcard type. I got a strong sense of this when the three teaching mediums filed out onto the minstrel-type gallery above the lady presenter who was sitting below and giving the introductions. They joked and quipped and gave a very brief demonstration of their skills. The vision of a giant, slightly macabre Punch and Judy show came into my mind.

It is me, my fault, I kept telling myself: my filters, my prejudice. This is the solid tradition of northern working class humour and humanity, facing up to tough times, helping each other out, making people feel at home, no airs and graces, puncturing pomposity. The audience was mainly middle-aged, female, and significantly overweight; except for one tall, portly, ex-military type with a cut glass accent, who stuck out. He, too, irritated me. It was no good. I was, like many ex-teachers and lecturers, hopeless at being taught. He was later paired with me in a small group activity and before we did some sensitivity enhancing exercises he told me about his guides.

Whoosh. I know when they are there. They settle — whoosh — on my spine, on the chakra.

We worked in pairs to sharpen our sensitivity to colour images by describing the effects that fabrics of different hues had on us. I looked at the material with pink roses on it and a cream background material,

Yearning, frivolous, champagny, I said.

I obviously wasn't, by the tone of my voice, taking the exercise seriously. He said, slightly uneasily,

I wouldn't use your words but I can see what you mean.

I had attended many conferences as part of my work and was used to good hotels and efficient facilities and organisation. I only lasted two of the four days on this course. It was held in a large rectangular room, with outside loos, and a couple of rooms at the back and in the basement for smaller group work and private sittings. You brought your own baps and sandwiches and mineral water, and donated a sum if you wanted grotty instant coffee at break times. There was a relentless atmosphere of fellowship and good cheer. Oh, my heart cried out to them, why do you make yourself so vulnerable to all the sharp shits in the media?

And yet they were right and I was wrong — yearning for my air-conditioned seminar and powerpoint presentation and three course buffet lunch. I knew that in my heart and really warmed to the sisters who ran the course — the elder of the two was a tiny, intense dark woman, dressed in blue, with sharp pain-ridden eyes (she had had much illness my sister told me), whose talks were full of tart yet insightful humour.

There were excellent presentations from David Fontana (a psychologist and one of the leading psychical researchers in the UK) and his colleague Anabela Cardoso (who had made a detailed study of electronic voice production). They were academics and middle class, fluent, enthusiastic, articulate, open to psychic activity, but not gullible. I was very impressed. But had a member of the press — at which end, tabloid or broadsheet, it didn't matter — been present they would have made mincemeat of the sessions on the development of mediumship. To see one medium after another — usually an overweight, middle-aged woman — go to the front and give a short demonstration of ineffable vagueness, and full of twists and turns as they hunted for the spirit link, was very depressing.

My sister and her husband attended part of the course and I took them out for a meal in a swanky part of town. The contrast in environments sharpened my frustrations and over the food I gave vent to them, but,

You don't understand, she said. These women are welcomed in Spiritualist churches wherever they go, and they bring money into the movement.

But, but, but, I wanted to say-but didn't.

In complete contrast were the visits from 2006 to 2010 to Cambridge. Anne loved the cycling, the architecture, the museums and art galleries. I did research in the Wren Library at Trinity College and the Society for Psychical Research archives in the Cambridge University Library (that rather threatening totalitarian structure designed by Gilbert Scott). These visits often seemed to coincide with periods of intense heat, but I stuck doggedly to it and got deeply into the Myers records and, on our last two visits, the materials relating to a further research project on the cross-correspondences (see Part 2). I loved the Wren — with its pale busts of brilliant men symbolising the richness of Trinity's intellectual tradition; the rituals of archival scholarship (when to use gloves, the correct way to open and support a fragile document, etc.); and the sense of personal tension (or affection or animosity who knows) touching but never quite breaking the surface of the library staff's hushed, almost silky interactions with each other.

Anne and I would meet up in the evening, each of us full of the day's discoveries. It was another stage in our increasing closeness, and in some painful but tender way was almost a gift from Ralph—though it, and all the writing and research, had been bought at such a price.

2007

In 2007 we had another few days in London and I was able to book a sitting at the College of Psychic Studies with one of their legendary star performers. The first part of the session covered material I had not expected since it basically involved an examination of my aura. I have not included that material here.

Sitting with medium 7 (male)
28.6.2007. Trevor present. London.

Your grandmother in spirit here	True
She assures you, you will always have enough	Pred
Concern about your mother's knees/joints	True
Previously very active	True
Your father is here	True
English reserve	True
Clean shoes	True
A proud man	True
Wants to help his children	Other
Piano in background	Other
Two dogs	Other
Your parents weren't Romeo and Juliet	True
You will be going to Spain	Pred
Finances better in 2008	Pred
Why so many sale signs?	Other
He was a generous man	True
You are a methodical man	True
You like things in the right place	True
I walk into your house	

The sitting room is on the right	True
It is sunny and safe	True
Why don't you feel secure?	True
At 68 you will be more chilled out	Pred
You are a good communicator	True
But I have to work to make friends with you	True
Your wife is very good with people	True
You have it in you to achieve as a writer	Pred
Two unfinished manuscripts now	True
All in all five by five years from today	Pred
You need more confidence	True
You have got the ability	Pred
Links with South Africa	False
Links with the South Coast of England	True
Paper work is piling up	True
But you don't need help	
You are your own critic	True
Love the inner man more	True
You will be published and successful	Pred
Your father is an honest man	True
What you see is what you get	True
He is getting to know his own father	Other
Why was last Xmas flat?	True
There are links to Yorkshire	Pred
Your writing is a mixture of historical fact and fiction	True
Your father couldn't say goodbye	True
He was a punctual man	True
He liked sitting in gardens	False
Who is Robert?	False
Your mum's dad comes	True
How can I help the boy?	Other
Also your father-in-law	True
Bit more tactile than your father	True
He is keeping an eye on his children	Other
October birthdays and anniversaries?	False
The date 22nd of November is important	True
There is a young man here	True

There is a strong bond with you	True
He is either a brother or a son	
A son	True
He, too, wants to help	Other
He died very quickly	True
You saw his body	True
You touched him or kissed him	True
Still have his clothes	True
V good sense of humour	True
Why Battle of Hastings? Ah, William the Conqueror	
You, too, will conquer in what you want to do	Pred
Your son was tactile	True
Glad your knee is better	True
His death was written about	True
What do you wear of his?	True
I am in your sitting room	
At least two portraits of him here	True
There is a cheesy aroma – he liked cheese	True
There is strength and gentleness in him	True
He had very expressive eyes	True
There is a mark above his eyebrows	False
He is still loving and looking after you both	Other
He is proud that you will be a noted author	Pred
One book of yours has 24 chapters	True
Cut it down and the waffle	True
He was interested in writing and literature	True
You also cook. He has memories of you cooking	True
You have things to achieve and you still have time to do it	Pred
He says tell my mother I am not dead	Other
There is a breeze in your sitting room	
Have you French doors, French windows?	True
He liked seeing bright orange flowers through the windows	Other
Sees you signing a contract	True
You gave him love and trust now he is giving it to you	Other
Your house is harmonious and lived in not a sanctuary	True
So many people in spirit coming	Other
Lady on your wife's side – died of cancer	True

He says Dad always had his head in a book	True
You have a mind that needs to be fed	True
You are very comfortable alone or in company	
You can take it or leave it	True
He liked company	True
People still talk about him	True
You can see your father and son as guardian angels if you like	Other
You have a good team around you	Other
You have just got to write. It will flow	Pred
You are the sort of person who can sit and work for five hours	True
Your son will help inspire you	Other
You have the sort of mind which one word or idea will set off	True
Have you a skin allergy? An itch?	False
From a mimosa tree?	False
Who is Simon?	True
Who is Mark?	True
There is a man you are comfortable with and whom you talk to	True
I have an image of you flying a kite	True
Just childhood memories	
Your life is nowhere near over yet	
You will achieve	Pred
Is there a problem with your digestion?	False
He had a sensitive stomach	True
He had ants in his pants and was very energetic	True
Death was not his fault	False
He liked animals	True
He had a very nice way of smiling	True
What is this about socks and socks to throw away?	True
Paper around you	True
You like everything at your fingertips	True
Success in later life is more appreciated and savoured	Pred
He is very proud of you and has faith in you	Other
It is already a done deal he thinks	Pred
Lake Como will have spiritual significance for you in the future	Pred

You have mood swings	True
You are very patterned – meaning a time for this and a time for that	True
You had a good upbringing	True
And have a lot of good things to achieve	Pred
You have so much to say. Release it	Pred
Your work will be easy to translate into film, to radio	Pred
You can paint pictures with words	Pred
They wouldn't waste time pushing you if you didn't know how to write	Pred
I get a scarf – associated with/belonging to your son?	True
There is an ornament you have put away	True
Looks like a fairy with butterfly wings	True
He liked it	True
Just a way of saying he hasn't left	Other
Your wife can also be very good at writing	True
You could be more romantically attentive	True
You have a strong-minded family in spirit	Other
Spiritual without the religious trappings	Other
Your father says you have six siblings	True
He is pouring out wine. Enjoy your wine	Other
You will have more than enough for all of your needs	Pred
Who sings?	Other
Your son listens to your wife singing	True
Your house is lived in. It has a nice, reassuring energy	True
Links with Mexico? Latin America?	True
There is still a market for interesting work	Pred
Who is Jane? There is a link with this name and the publishing of your books	Pred

The assessment of the sitting with medium 7

This sitting was probably the most unusual of them all. The medium had a Mediterranean background and came to England as a child and, though very fluent in English, still paused and fretted slightly while he tried to get the exact word. He was charming and courteous but could also be very direct at times, confident that he had the charm to get away with it. The material came in great rushes with sudden changes of focus. There were a small number of clear errors and some hits of great precision. The description of my character and interests was accurate, as were those of my father and Ralph. Ralph had been fascinated as a child by an outside light in the shape of an angel with wings. It had been put outside the front door of two of our houses. There were 24 chapters in my draft biography of Myers and they needed to be cut and weeded. I had never counted them before. I did have six siblings. My mother's birthday was on the 22nd of November. I did fly a kite for Ralph as a child on one particularly memorable occasion.

The description of the nature of my writing was partially accurate. My current research and writing at that time was purely historical. However, as a relief from the intricacies of psychical research, I was also researching and doing some early drafting of a spy novel set in 1940. That, if it ever comes to fruition, will be a mixture of fact and fiction. Whether it will have the impressive qualities outlined above is rather unlikely!

The question of fishing came up strongly in this sitting largely because of the medium's slightly cheeky and teasing approach. However, there was only one occasion where I felt that he used my response to get himself going again. Generally, he seemed to plug into his source after a pause for breath and the information would come in an energetic flurry. Much of the information appeared to be coming pictorially and it was up to him to make sense of the images. The sitting was a blend of the psychic and the mediumistic: partly encouragement for me to have more faith in myself and believe that I could achieve as a writer and that I would (predictive statements to that effect), and partly statements of survival evidence.

2008

This year the pressure (admittedly self-inflicted) increased as I struggled to knock the Myers manuscript into some halfway acceptable shape. This meant spending a considerable amount of time at my study desk and continually jumping up and down to dig out and verify references from the rapidly accumulating black box files on the shelves above and the floor below. My desk and computer were very close to the window that looked down the main village street and I sometimes worried that my frequent appearances in the window would lead some people to suspect me of voyeuristic tendencies. In fact I had read somewhere that the police had checked out a writer — briefly — whose desk was situated in a very similar position to mine. I mentioned this to Anne but she thought, as usual, that I was being over imaginative. However, in May of that year I was bending and standing by the window sorting the files and trying to hoover up the dust that had accumulated when I noticed a woman staring at me across the way and she continued to stare for a number of seconds longer. A day or two later I half smiled at a girl and her father who were measuring something in a garden. It was a smile of sympathy since she seemed so bored. Yet he looked at me with hostility and about a week after that a car slowed threateningly right down beside me and then accelerated away. I had no idea who it was since I was going to the post and had the wrong glasses on. All this was mildly disturbing and seemed to be reinforced by other silly little incidents and from stray comments that I heard floating up over our wall

That's where X lives and that's where the weird guy lives

It appeared that a number of people thought that way. Yet Anne and I had made good and warm friends in the village and the vast majority of people were pleasant and courteous. What was going on?

Anne said I was misinterpreting things and it was just a product of overwork. I was not so sure but did not know what to do. I can remember glaring, after a couple of glasses at a party, at someone whom I thought, irrationally, might have been party to spreading rumour and gossip, and realised the following morning that I had better knock these feelings on the head. I decided the best thing, psychologically, was to use the situation to help me sharpen my sense of what evidence was and see if the exercise could assist me in my assessment of mediumship material.

The first point was that these people, whoever they were and if they existed, were victims of cognitive framing. That is, they saw me at the window, and would see me there regularly as I was almost always at my desk and, as an architect friend pointed out, our house was a visual focal point for everyone travelling north through the village. They, not knowing my reason for being in the window, or unfamiliar with an historian's constant need to check and verify references, would, depending on their own preconceptions, project a particular meaning on to the incident and judge all future events/incidents associated with me in the same way.

I also noticed in myself an occasional tendency to anxiety in social and public situations which sometimes led me to act in a slightly panicky way. I looked the syndrome up and it is not uncommon but I found it embarrassing. Two examples: we went to Madrid for a short break. It was at a time of heightened Basque terrorist threat. Anne had taken a taxi back to the hotel from the railway station which we had looked round but I decided to walk, as I always did in interesting cities. I tried to find a lavatory and also a piece of paper that Anne said she might have dropped in the station. As I walked around I suddenly realised this was where there had been a terrible bombing a few years before. Maybe the CCTV people thought I was a terrorist appraising the situation. I walked quickly out and hurried back to the hotel but bumped into a whole load of policemen obviously waiting for the cavalcade of some bigwig to pass by. This made me move even faster and this, plus my need to urinate and also to try to find my way back to the hotel, made my behaviour rather jerky and erratic. I eventually made the hotel but fretted for several days that I might be under observation.

The second incident was a domestic and rural one. A woman put vegetables out at the end of the village and in a docile rural community purchasers were trusted to leave the correct money in a jam jar. That day, I got into a complete mess over the money. I had bought a variety of vegetables and couldn't remember whether I'd put too much or too little in. There were a couple of men up a ladder on the neighbouring house. Absurdly, I thought they might think that this guy had not paid the full amount for his vegetables. So, I went to the house closest to the grass verge where the vegetables were left (thinking, not unnaturally, that it was her house) to explain that I would make up the money if she was short and that she could keep any money if she was over. It was not her house, and trying to explain to the owner what I was doing knocking on his door was very embarrassing.

Some considerable time later I was in a supermarket in the city. At the checkout a woman in another aisle and closer to the till than me turned her head and our eyes met briefly. She looked startled and afraid and then, taking her purchases, literally ran out of the store. Did she think I was stalking her? She appeared to recognise me but I had never seen her before in my life. Again, Anne put it all down to my over-active imagination and said she was probably worried that her parking ticket had expired.

I drew two conclusions from all this. One for me: in all these cases I felt myself being observed and my motives impugned and my, potentially, being accused unjustly of something. Was this a legacy of my father's criticism from childhood? The universe seemed to be unfair and unfriendly. Was my investigation into mediumship just a rather cowardly attempt to reassure myself that all would ultimately be well? If they were misjudging me, because of certain fears and false assumptions, maybe I was misjudging the statements the mediums made, because of a longing for the security of survival? Did this mean that I ignored evidence unfavourable to the survival hypothesis and exaggerated material favourable to it? I decided, therefore, in the write up not to provide a summary of the sittings, but to put down all the transcripts in statement form so as to allow independent readers the opportunity to make a full judgment. In addition, I went over the tapes at regular intervals to see if I had missed any relevant material that I might subconsciously have suppressed.

There was also an aspect of all this which was relevant to the process of mediumship itself. Caught up in my states of social anxiety (particularly the two incidents described above), my perceptions of what was going on seemed convincing to me at the time. Were there any clues from this as to how mediums might generate a plausible sense of contact with discarnate personalities? Could I, by analysing my own experience, detect the psychological mechanisms involved in mediumship? These episodes made me think about the nature of sanity—particularly issues of hallucination, misperception, and the kinds of people and kinds of states that might encourage such phenomena. So, as well as looking carefully at myself and the way I was interpreting the evidence, I also needed to examine the mediums' statements, turns of phrases, and interaction with me. Were they deceiving themselves as well as me? Were they in a 'normal' state when receiving communications, or in a state of mild or moderate dissociation? To what extent were the statements they made, no matter how convincing, merely a form of storytelling or play acting?

We visited London in November 2008 and stayed again near the British Museum, and once more I looked forward to exploring the area. The Swedenborg Centre was not far away and there was a New Age bookshop nearby where I could sometimes pick up rare and interesting first editions of early psychical research texts. I had booked in two sessions, one at the SAGB in the morning and one in the afternoon at the CPS. I wandered down past the National Portrait Gallery and through Pall Mall across Green Park and on to the SAGB: as ever, I marvelled at its incongruous situation in the heart of plush Belgravia redolent with late-Victorian and Edwardian associations of Oscar Wilde and Lily Langtry. It was rather shabby and down at heel behind its impressive facade—all fur coat and no knickers as my grandmother might have said, after a British sherry or two. I also found it amusing that both the Royal College of Psychiatrists and the Spiritualist Association of Great Britain were in Belgrave Square, and sometimes wondered what they made of each other and whether there was any communication between them.

Sitting with medium 8 (female)
5.11.2008. Trevor present. London.

I sat in a cramped waiting room with two other people, an elderly man and an Indian lady in a sari. The medium fetched me. She set the tape going having first ascertained that I had had sittings before and knew what to expect. She was a young, intelligent, open faced woman, possibly of Spanish origin, and of medium height.

Link on Mother's side building up	True
Small, elegant	True
Everything by the book	True
Church in her life	False
Passed over with debilitating disease	True
You have healing ability	False
With words	False
Special link with mother	True
Anniversary around now	True
Lots of changes for you	True
You've just been joined by a lady with a sari	Other
You are very much a thinker	True
You will be bringing in new projects	True
Lots of energy and time	True

Though retired you are busier than ever	True
The foundation of your personality is colour	Other
I have never seen this before	
Colour is very important in your life	False
Spirit people are filling your head with information	Other
You will be encountering people with unusual gifts	Pred
Your destiny is to teach and talk and to instruct others	Pred
You have a lot to share with humanity	Pred
This lady is from Delhi	Other
A link with your father	Other
Someone is being really awkward	Other
I am seeing a board	False
Also an extremely intelligent soul	Other
He is pushing the boundaries of your intelligence	Other
Not just logically	Other
Next three months will be challenging	True
Travel to different countries	Pred
India is a possibility in 2009	False
The only person here is on a mother link	True
You can't summon spirit. They often use dreams	Other
And you are lucky you can smell smoke	True
I can see silver lights on your father's side	Other
He is supporting/influencing your work	Other
You will be very successful	Pred
Your work is also healing you	True
Is there a priest in the family?	Other

The assessment of the sitting with medium 8

There was a notice at the reception desk of the SAGB which stated that you could claim your money back only if in the first few minutes of the session it was clear that the statements were not meaningful at all. I should have done this, but for experimental purposes I decided to let the sitting run. One might be able to learn as much from unsuccessful sittings as good ones (so counselled my rational man), but my emotional side was feeling pretty miffed. Apart from the points about hard work and challenges which were true and perhaps a little (though by no means highly) unusual for a man of my age, the rest seemed largely drivel and just plain wrong. The only thing that gave me pause was the point about smelling smoke, which both Anne and I had done on occasion after Ralph's death.

On later analysis of the tape I noticed three general points. Firstly, because she seemed to be off target I (typical middle class politeness I suppose) started to talk more. But if she was a cold reader she didn't seem to be particularly good at it. Secondly, as our session faded out, I asked her about the processes of mediumship as she saw them. She said that originally she saw images in her mind's eye but as she gained in skill and experience she saw misty external figures (as if covered in a muslin screen), the mother's side on the right of the sitter and the father's side on the left, and that no one could summon them. They would come as they wished or not and that in my case there was a direct link through dreams. True, I did dream about Ralph a lot. However, it seemed a rather convenient get out. Thirdly, I could, with a little ingenious thought, make sense of some of the puzzling statements. But I decided that anything that required complex effort of that nature to make it fit should be discarded, and I kept to this principle through all the readings.

I then hurried down to Kensington, irritated by the session, snatched a quick sandwich and mineral water, taken on the run, rushed past the Victoria and Albert Museum, and made the College of Psychic Studies just in time for my next sitting. This was hardly the best state in which to arrive. However, the sitting, after the wispy farrago in the morning, was to stun me.

Sitting with medium 9 (male)
5.11.2008. Trevor present. London.

I found the medium to be a very open and straightforward young man with a South London accent, neatly dressed in dark suit without tie. I had forgotten the tape and asked him to wait while I went back to reception to fetch it. He started at once after putting the tape in. There was the usual box of white tissues on a small table nearby.

Gentleman pacing up and down believer in punctuality	True
Spic and span in a good way	True
Collar and tie regimented highly polished shoes	True
His way of dealing with you was pull your socks up	True
Not a good patient at the end	False
Better at dispensing advice than taking it	True
Razor sharp mind	True
Mainly facts and figures	True
Distanced himself from people	True
Lack of mobility towards the end	True
November has a lot of meanings for him	True
Didn't like gossip/flowery language	True
Get to the point	True
Falling out with a family male figure of his generation	True
Too stubborn	True
Never said sorry	True
You've had a lot to deal with in the past 2/3 years	True
Sometimes wondered who to turn to	True
Your instinct is to buckle down	True
The name Mary or Margaret	True
Also something significant in July around Independence Day	True
A legacy of self-doubt from criticism in youth	True
But you have coped with it	True
He wasn't a good listener	True
You are more polite but you need to listen more	True
He's showing me pots/archaeology/a dig/	
Broken bits fit together to get information out	True
Very important for you	Pred
You have a large knowledge that you need to share	Pred
Don't be put off by self-doubt or being too hard on yourself	Other
There is a connection to America work/business which is building	Pred
There are Scottish connections in the family	True
There is a naval link	Other

Dog in spirit/ Labrador or a setter	True
A man's dog	True
More mellow since he's learnt a lot on that side	Other
You felt isolated at school and he did not understand	True
He saw sensitivity as a weakness not a strength	True
He apologises	Other
He was too harsh and unforgiving	True
Medals and things of this sort emotionally important to him	True
He had his routine and didn't want to be disturbed	True
Learned a lot from watching you re tolerance and supportiveness	Other
A lady here	False
Died exhausted in mid-seventies	False
Difficult childhood	False
I have a young man here	True
Died suddenly	True
Upbeat person who lifted spirits when he walked into a room	True
He's been about you a lot recently	Other
Just in the next room	Other
He didn't always see the dangers and pitfalls in things	True
Regretted not having more conversations with you Which he enjoyed	True
Sees you working with your head down	True
You over-do it at times	True
Next Spring is an important period	True
He had humour and a quick wit	True
Very popular	True
He had a good send off like a pop star. I made my mark	True
Very compassionate person	True
Championed the underdog	True
Knowledge of words and love of the arts	True
Incident to do with your coat	True
Decision to be made next year with a further project And projects after that	True
He'll try to help	Other
Go with instinct not knowledge	Other
You have a link with French/French history to do with work	True

Don't lose contact with people. You can be isolated	True
Someone playing a cello/stringed instrument?	True
He had wisdom at a young age	True
Felt 2/3 years older than his school friends	True
Thanks you for allowing him to flourish and grow in his own way	True
Even though he pushed the boundaries	True
Don't be impatient	Other
There are good things to come from your work	Pred
What you have wanted is coming	Pred
You will have a period of sharp pains in the ears	Pred
Also a whistling sound	Pred
Watch out for it	

The assessment of the sitting with medium 9

Apart from the session with medium 1 this was the sitting which I found the most convincing on an emotional level but which, paradoxically, later left me with a nagging residual sense of doubt. He spoke very quickly and clearly and without much hesitation. The sitting was virtually one hundred percent accurate with regard to my father's character and personality. Medals were important to him and we have a picture of him, with my mother and youngest sister, very smart and polished, in the appropriate dress, outside Buckingham Palace after receiving his MBE from the Queen. The medium seemed to lose his way in the middle with his description of a woman in her seventies who died exhausted and had a difficult childhood. But he returned to form with an accurate description of Ralph.

He, too, ended with certain predictions which I will discuss later.

2009

My Myers biography came out in this year and in that broad sense the predictions from several mediums that I would be published were fulfilled. I was also fortunate in that year and early in the following one to gain additional research funding to start on an investigation of the cross-correspondences and to visit archives in America. So again, for what it is worth, another prediction was fulfilled. I did visit America and some financial pressure was taken off me—*you will always have enough*. However, the mysterious Jane who will help in the publication of my books has not yet materialised and I doubt that she ever will!

I also had the very enjoyable experience of lecturing on Myers at the National Portrait Gallery, my lecture coinciding with a small exhibition of his wife Eveleen's photographs there. She was a significant figure, along with Julia Margaret Cameron (whom she knew), in the history of Victorian photography.

2010

April

Early in the year I had a sudden shock—the kind that every writer dreads. My left eye seemed to have become very fuzzy and weak. I had been diagnosed with glaucoma—in both eyes—around 2000, but I had administered the eye drops regularly and the rate of decline had seemed very gradual. However, after examination it was recommended I have a trabulectomy to further reduce the pressure in the left eye. I was, of course, concerned, but realised I had been provided with an excellent opportunity to experiment with alternative methods of healing at no risk to myself. We had intended to take a week's break in Norfolk since we loved the great skies and wide beaches of the region with their edgings of dark pine. I discovered that Matthew Manning, as famous in his time as Uri Geller, had a healing practice in Suffolk and that glaucoma was one of the conditions he thought he could make some impression on. We could drop in on the way.

He had based himself in a moated country house of some considerable charm. The owners let him use the library for the healing and the great hall for reception and administration. They also did up-market bed and breakfast so Anne and I stayed there as well.

The following morning I went down to my first session. It was a lovely bright day with a low wind. Manning's secretary was very warm and relaxed and we had a pleasant conversation about Matthew's remarkable gifts and how many people he had helped. The owners, when we talked to them later about this, also confirmed (and they had had no special faith in alternative medicine before) the tributes paid to Matthew from many of the patients who had visited. I went in for my session. The library was a pleasant room, now more a family sitting room than a library, with a powerful stove-like fire at one end, photographs and family items on one wall, and books, at the opposite end of the room to the fire, on dogs, horses, and country pursuits that firmly reflected the squirearchical lineage of the family who had owned the property for centuries. The treatment consisted of a sustained series of passes close to my eyes, head, and neck. I felt considerable warmth emanating from his hands and both relaxed and energised as I took my breaks during the day.

As he began the healing again in the afternoon session he said (for there is a touch of the showman in him and no harm in that)

Right, fasten your safety belt.

Instantly there flashed into my mind the vivid image of having dreamt all this before—me in the chair by a roaring fire, a man bending over me and using that very phrase. At the end of the session he said that the healing could well take a couple of months to have full effect. I felt very relaxed and tingling and went to sit in the sun under one of the great trees till Anne returned.

At dinner that night we discussed the situation. I had had a very interesting experience but I was not going to postpone or refuse the trabulectomy unless the pressures in my eyes when later tested, and some tangible, measurable improvement in my left eye, were noted. But the date for the operation came so hard on the heels of the visit that I felt it would be foolish not to go through with it anyway. So I did. However, shortly after the session with Matthew, and before the operation, I was delighted to pass the special driving eye test to allow me to continue driving, but I have to keep an open mind about which intervention was the most effective and which would have the most long-term benefit. However, I liked Manning a lot and thought him warm, genuine, and intelligent. He was ambivalent about many, though by no means all, parapsychologists, partly because of their dismissive attitude towards the strange phenomena that clustered around him in adolescence.

October

We went to London for a little fun and a little culture and I also wanted to do some research in the Harry Price Collection at Senate House (as ever looking like Superman's Metropolis). In addition, I had been invited to give a talk on Myers to the Ghost Club, which claimed its existence pre-dated the SPR. I was not sure that I needed or wanted another sitting with a medium, but I decided that as I was in London anyway it was worth a shot, and might give me another perspective.

The weather was clear and golden. Yet there was a certain menace in the air, as London was on high security alert for terrorist threats, and as I walked round Belgrave Square I noticed a very fit looking young man with his Range Rover parked nearby, twice giving me a careful look. I tried to keep my tendency to paranoia under control and went round the corner into the SAGB.

I noticed my medium (I recognised him from the photo gallery on the SAGB website) standing smoking in the foyer (hardly outside). He was with another medium who looked like a rather frayed jolly jack tar and who suddenly burst into raucous song of the O Sole Mio variety and then, poking his head outside, shouted

He's getting out of the taxi now and paying with a handful of fivers.

Obviously someone of importance was expected. As I turned to leave an impressively good looking young man walked imperiously in, and failed to acknowledge the fact that I had held the door open for him and had stood back courteously. I muttered

Thank YOU.

I immediately felt very Mr Pooter-ish. The scene was melodramatic, even surreal. There seemed to be something about the foyer and reception of the Spiritualist Association of Great Britain that attracted these heightened scenes and emotions. I remember a previous occasion when I had encountered a young widow (I assumed) dressed in elegant black, looking slightly stunned from her sitting. She seemed about to speak to me and then obviously thought better of it and moved away back in the direction of Hyde Park. And again, there was the man, who rushed in and shouted to the receptionist,

Quick. I want the best medium in the house. Now. And I don't care what it costs.

Such a contrast to the more genteel and middle class College of Psychic Studies when I visited — the team of courteous receptionists, the range of alternative therapies and approaches, the easily accessible library.

I said to the receptionist at the SAGB. What about the library?

We can't open it, she said. Too many books have been stolen and our insurers won't let us.

I looked shocked.

That's nothing, she said. They'll nick anything here. Soap, light bulbs, toilet paper from the lavatories, and anything that's not nailed down in the hall.

Surely not the sitters who've paid £35? No, it's those who come for the free services and clairvoyance on a Sunday and Wednesday.

Sitting with medium 10 (male)
10.10.2010. Trevor present. London.

I went a little depressed to my session, noticing as I sat in the waiting room that I could clearly hear the other medium with his client in the next room. The rooms seem to have been cheaply partitioned, not like the solidly built and spacious sitting rooms of the CPS.

I gave him the cassette for the recording.

Have you sat before?

Do you know what to expect?

Yes.

Have we sat before?

No.

I asked him about his history. He said he was naturally psychic from the age of 13 — it ran in the family. He stated he was mainly clairaudient. Spirits would speak very quickly to him and he would relay the messages. He asked me if I had any particular issues or concerns. I said no. This seemed to throw him a little and it immediately put me on my guard.

Lady has walked straight towards you. About 5'3" to 5'4"	False
Lovely looking skin for lady of her age	True
In her 80s	False
Suffered towards the end	True
Died without saying goodbye to everyone	True
Very soft-spoken woman	True
Got on well with people	True
Smiling and popular	True
But beneath surface problems which she kept hidden	True
Very independent	True
Embarrassed by help at end	True
Had looked after many people	True

Death a release	True
Much happier now	Other
Good looking in younger years if she says so herself	True
Not one for blowing her own trumpet	True
Not a lot of makeup	True
Flowers in your arms	Other
You were down the last month	True
Flowers for this	Other
She liked gardens and parks	True
You think all the time	True
You are a good man	Other
Give a lot without expecting things back	Other
Interesting pathway through life	True
Sees you in suit	False
Must be something coming	Pred
You learn fast and absorb info like a sponge	True
You make a lovely photo	Other
Suits in your closet now	False
3 suits in closet	Pred
You have mediumistic and healing powers	False
Connection in your family re this	True
It is building up	Pred
You are a modern day Sherlock	
After the truth	True
You have written a book	True
Many more things to come and to do	Pred
Also I get a mixture of photos large and small	True
Been to the States	True
And going back there again	True
She puts passport and ticket in the table	
It will be the bestest time of your life	Pred
Interesting results	Pred
You need a dictaphone for the trip	Other
Do a checklist for the trip	True
I see a link to magazines	
No, journals	True
You get on with most people	True

But if not you show it in your face	True
You are old fashioned and modern at the same time	True
Like father on outside and mother inside	True
Emotions and pain kept the inside	True
This lady has been round you for a long time	Other
She has either made noises in house in past	Other
Or will in the future	Pred
Due for opticians	Pred
You need to check your teeth	Pred
Tension in head and neck and spine	False
You are going to be a busy, busy man	Pred
She wants you to make a documentary	Pred
You tried briefly	True
Pleasing results here	Pred
You have visited the spirit world at night	Other
And will do so again	Other
Dad on other side	True
A proud looking man	True
Not much height difference	True
Wonderful relationship since brings flowers	False
Lost his looks towards the end	True
Condensed milk colour	
Apologises for being harsh	True
Has respect for you	Other
Should be more like you	Other
Learnt by watching you	Other
Apologises to wife and sends love	Other
Not kind to a lot of people	True
Too sharp a tongue	True
He wants your name in lights	Other
You are confident and positive but sometimes dither	True
Get on with it	True
When you do no stopping you	Pred
Take capsules for bone joints and a glass of milk	True
More doorways opening	Pred
One in South Africa/Africa	Pred
Can he give you a hug	Other

No other footsteps in the room except these two	Other
Massive respect sent from your Dad	Other
Will give you a hug not love since didn't say it in life	Other

The assessment of the sitting with medium 10

He spoke rapidly with little hesitation. I found his language rather irritating at times — *you are going to be a busy, busy boy, bestest time ever* — a kind of slangy over-familiarity. However, an experienced cold reader, one would have thought, would have adjusted the language and vocabulary to the sitter. So this might count in his favour? The description of my grandmother was reasonably accurate though he had her about four inches too tall. The suits — I had worn suits for a significant part of my professional life but no longer did so and had no intention of going down that path again. The comments on my current research and the visit to America were accurate. What was suspicious was his capacity to switch tack when wrong (called 'forking' in cold reading terminology),

You haven't heard noises in the house? Well they are to come —

Not a wonderful relationship with your father? Well, he has a great respect for you.

Pretty mind-numbing too were statements to the effect that I got on with most people and that I should do a checklist for my American visit (which in fact I was about to do). This seemed to be like low-level psychic reading, almost of the seaside/funfair/village fete-type, than the higher quality experiences I had had before.

Medium 10 said that he was clairaudient and I found the phrase, when I asked him if there was anyone else there, *no other footsteps in the room*, moving and poetic, but also baffling at the same time. What actually was he hearing and where was it located? I consider this and related questions in Part 2.

November/December

After Ralph's death we anticipated every November and December with real dread. His birthday was in November, as was Anne's, and mine was in December, and then there was the misery of the Christmas period. However, one of the things that kept Anne and me going through these times was humour. Sometimes we could distance ourselves from it all. Anne heard a poet on television saying that the death of his son was the most calamitous event in his life. She said is calamity the right word? Do we still use calamity in that sense? Surely a poet could have chosen a better word? We both felt that calamity—O Calamity, O Infamy, Infamy, they've all got it in for me—had a touch of the Carry On Films now, or of Calamity Jane. It reminded us, too, how we discovered that the undertaker had misspelled tragedy in his first draft of the notice of Ralph's death to go in the local paper—surely this was one of the essential pieces of training at undertaker school?

However, although Ralph's death brought us closer together, there was one tendency in myself that I had to watch carefully in case it distressed Anne. I was caught up in the great game, the mighty quest, the fascination of the search for life after death and the attractiveness, originality, and complexity of many personalities who had gone down this trail before me. This meant that I would sometimes come running to her like a dog who had just brought the morning paper in between his teeth—look what I've got—momentarily forgetting the fact that Ralph wasn't a piece in a hugely complex jigsaw puzzle, he was her Ralph. She also found it difficult to accept, as I have mentioned, that I, over the years, had a number of very vivid and comforting dreams in which he played a central part. She did not have dreams like these for a long time and thought, most unfairly to herself, that she had offended him in some way and that he was punishing her for it, and blamed herself for some of their spats and quarrels in his late teens and early adulthood. And, occasionally, though she fought hard against it, the physical grotesqueness of it all broke through. She came to me once after she had tended his grave;

That beautiful boy. I had a sudden thought of him still there a few feet below as I changed the flowers.

Even nine years later it could still suddenly overwhelm us, rising from an apparently calm sea.

I was lucky, as I have said, in my frequent dream contact with him. For example, I had a particularly vivid one of him on the night of Wednesday 24th Nov 2010. In golden light we met at the top of the stairs. We embraced and he stroked the side of my face—where I had recently been diagnosed with a pre-cancerous growth and which was shortly to be operated on. And then I tried the experiment of mentally asking Ralph to communicate with Anne in dreams and, to our delight (but with absolutely no evidential value attached to it), she began to, shortly before Christmas that year.

So, as the years went by and more and more evidence accumulated (patchy though some of it was) from different mediums, a cautious belief in the possibility of survival (no more) gradually began to grow in me. However, this was moderated by the increasing depth and breadth of my reading and, therefore, my greater appreciation of the range of issues involved. I remember visiting one of the leading elder statesmen in the field of psychical research in the UK (he was going, very kindly, to lend me some important research materials). Over lunch I asked him breezily,

Well, do you believe in life after death?

He gave me a look composed, I now think, partly of polite irritation that I had posed such a simple question and partly of curiosity to see whether I had the mettle to find out why the question was not as simple as it seemed. To unpacking the complexity of that deceptively straightforward question I now turn.

PART 2

Reflections

How was I going to make sense of what these mediums told me? Could I really believe any of it? Were they conning me? Could they tell by my appearance, accent, vocabulary, and reaction to their words what sort of person I was? In some moods I could easily understand and sympathise with the statements that down to earth and sceptical people might make on this subject. For example, Nicholas Humphrey (1996) has written that mediums don't communicate in a straightforward way but in enigmatic statements and that they steal information from the sitter (*ibid.*: 133). His description seems a parody of my/our most remarkable sittings and possibly betrays a lack of awareness of the best literature and research on the subject, or at least an engagement with it in sufficient depth.

His attitude is understandable, however, and reflects the general assumption of many people that if you consulted a medium after bereavement, and began to think there was something it, your cognitive faculties were impaired by grief and you were both conned and deluded. Anne and I were particularly sensitive to this charge of 'magical thinking' when we began to smell Ralph's characteristic cigarette smoke, and when the light outside his bedroom spectacularly performed even when switched off. We were delighted to read that such effects were quite widely reported. There are good examples of these electrical anomalies and other similar phenomena in Wright's book (2002). She started to investigate these things when the powerful lamp her partially-sighted husband had read by flashed and flickered in a kind of Morse code after his death (Wright, 2002: 2–8).

This fear, bluntly, of being seen as bonkers is strongly reinforced by the prevailing rationalist zeitgeist. The mind is so obviously merely the brain in action, and with the death of brain and body goes all individual consciousness for good. Stokes (1993), for example, who is sympathetic to certain aspects of psi, finds it impossible to accept survival of the existing personality because of the considerable and consistent body of evidence that links the functioning and effectiveness of the human personality with the health of brain and body. He gives the example of the disastrous impact of damage to the hippocampal and thalamic areas on the capacity for new long-term memory storage. And for many people, too, the effect of Alzheimer's on a loved one's personality and performance is conclusive proof of the mind's total dependence on the body. The nature of consciousness seems so fragile, as Zeman has pointed out (2002: 149–51). It needs oxygen, glucose, clean blood, adequate sleep, electrical equilibrium, etc. or it fails. It can be very easily disrupted or interrupted or obliterated, and it can be incredibly difficult to detect either in absence or presence. In addition, the development of neuroscience and functional magnetic resonance imaging has reinforced this view with their emphasis on mapping the brain and the identification of centres in the brain where particular functions appear to reside.

This has led to a rather over-simplistic belief in the explanatory power of fMRI, and Tallis (2011) has written vigorously on this. He has pointed out the seductive and persuasive appeal of blood-oxygen-level-dependent MRI. An increase in the activity of neurons is associated with an increase in oxygen to the nearby blood vessels. This can give a visual idea of which part of the brain is utilised when someone is engaged in a physical or mental process. This is useful in that neuronal activity lasts milliseconds whereas changes in blood flow occur over a longer and more easily identified period. This has led to claims that we have found where love, spirituality, wisdom, criminality, etc. may reside in the brain. Highly valuable though this technique is for many diagnostic purposes, it is, according to Tallis, misleading if applied, without due discrimination, to the processes and nature of consciousness. For, as Tallis points out, the crucial neuronal activity may go undetected; the experiments themselves tend to measure responses to very simple stimuli when, in fact, our emotions and the real-world contexts in which we operate are very complex; and finally, the point that there is a correlation of blood flow with particular functions does not necessarily mean one causing the other or being identical to the other. In addition, as Eagleman (2011) has stressed, there is nothing in current neuroscience that rules out a transmissive theory of consciousness, as William James proposed in the 1890s — namely that our neural circuitry (rather like a radio or a television set) picks up signals (consciousness) which essentially reside outside the brain (*ibid.*: 220–23).

It should be stressed, however, that the mere fact that an eminent scientist or doctor severely criticises some materialistic interpretations, because of their naïve lack of appreciation of the full range of issues involved, does not mean they can be automatically enrolled in the 'Spiritualist' or 'dualist' camp. Tallis is a humanist and atheist, and Hacker, one of the joint authors of a magnificent and challenging book, *Philosophical Foundations of Neuroscience* (Bennett and Hacker, 2003), while being severely critical of an atomistic and reductive approach, nevertheless denies the existence of the non-physical.

However, regardless of the niceties and subtleties of the strengths and weaknesses of fMRI scans, the attitude of professional scientists is fully understandable. For example, the entry in the *Penguin Dictionary of Psychology* on parapsychology mentions that 'the majority of psychologists are deeply sceptical and for good reason' about the paranormal.

The reasons given are sound and must be addressed. Firstly, it is 'notoriously difficult' to replicate paranormal phenomena. Secondly, they challenge the known and trusted laws of science. Thirdly, there is no body of established theory that effectively explains these incidents, relates them to the existing scientific paradigm, or modifies that paradigm in a way that is testable across a number of laboratories. Fourthly, fraud and self-delusion have been very strongly associated with this area. I will examine these points in some detail later. Finally, there is a pecking order within the sciences themselves, as Becher and Trowler make clear (2001). Psychology, itself so sniffy about the status of parapsychology, can itself be sniffed at!

On the other hand, many researchers over the years have made the point that the laboratory-based approach may not be the most effective and appropriate way of investigating paranormal forces and events. Secondly, regardless of the difficulties and complexities involved, it is unscientific to ignore awkward anomalies that have a habit of popping up, unpredictably, time and again. Science starts with observation and a nagging curiosity about those things that just don't fit. Professor Ian Stevenson (2008) has pointed out the often amusing stubbornness of some scientists in refusing to consider either phenomena which are not easily and repeatedly observable, or new inventions that *a priori* are ruled out as fraudulent or impossible. He cites Lavoisier's dismissal of the existence of meteorites, the initial rejection of Pasteur's work on microbes, and the early hostility to the phonograph and the telephone, amongst others. The demonstrator of Edison's phonograph before the Paris Academy of Sciences was accused of being a mere ventriloquist and almost physically assaulted.

The attitude of the Christian Churches has been hardly more positive. Brought up as an Anglican and going through some of their various rites of passage, I have frequently come across the unease that practising Christians and their clergy display when someone innocently raises the question of the nature of life after death and whether there is anything in mediumship at all. Christian theologians like Richard Swinburne, for example, tend to base their arguments on philosophical and theological grounds and ignore the empirical evidence from psychical research (Swinburne, 2004). In general, responses are often on the following lines. The first reaction is often that something indelicate has been said. The second is, sadly, sometimes bluster or patronisation. The third is often semi-superstitious — a grave warning about dabbling in unknown forces, occasionally combined with Biblical prohibitions on the subject. All these responses are usually based on a complete ignorance of the history and literature of the field.

However, another approach, rare, but hopefully growing, is the effort of thoughtful and open-minded Christians to explore these phenomena, to build bridges, and to incorporate the results in an expanded and generous theology. Examples of this are the practical explorations of David Kennedy, the Church of Scotland minister whose experiences I refer to later in the text; the writings of Bishop Hugh Montefiore (2002); the low key and sensitive work of the Churches' Fellowship for Psychical and Spiritual Studies; the seminal books of John Hick (1976, 2004); the positive attitudes of some Catholic priests to the phenomenon of electronic voice production; and the recent Australian journal *The Ground of Faith*, available on the internet. Unfortunately these attempts to build bridges have not always been helped by the attitude of some Spiritualists who see religion as a negative and persecuting force and who adopt a fiercely anti-clerical approach to organised religion. One can sympathise with the attitude, given the hostility and ignorance mentioned above. But it makes bridge-building more difficult.

Philosophers, too, (with honourable exceptions) are reluctant to take the question seriously. They either argue that the concept of the survival of a disembodied individual self is intellectually incoherent (Flew, 1953) and/or they assert that Hume, in his section X of *An Enquiry concerning Human Understanding,* has said all that needs to be said about the empirical absurdity of the miraculous and the paranormal. The argument is that as we have wide ranging and consistent evidence that there is uniformity in nature (events are natural not miraculous), we must weigh that carefully against the supposed miracle, even if we are the individual who has experienced it. Whenever we have explored these things in depth we have found a natural cause. Therefore, the presumption must be that we always will. Sidgwick, as President of the Society for Psychical Research in its early, formative years, powerfully argued against this position, stating that substantial and carefully assessed evidence could weigh against the improbability of miracles (Hamilton, 2009: 270).

There is also an objection that I have frequently encountered amongst well educated individuals—why do we always get ordinary people communicating trivia through mediums? Where are the messages from the great figures of the past? There are two obvious answers to this (without in any way coming down on either side of the survival debate). The first is that if such an individual has survived she/he might naturally be very chary about giving their name. It could sensationalise and discredit the whole process. Secondly, there are (again without prejudging the issue) plenty of examples of alleged communications from the great, the good, and not so good from the past. Oscar Wilde is supposed to have made contact with characteristic literary flourishes through the automatic writing of Hester Dowden. There is a brief account of this in the autobiography of Geraldine Cummins (1951: 116–22), but the interpretation of this set of episodes is particularly complex (Sidgwick, 1924). Matthew Manning produced some remarkable automatic paintings in the style of Dürer, Beardsley, etc. (Manning, 1974: 83–140), and Chico Xavier (a man of modest education) had written 'through him', *Parnassus from Beyond the Tomb,* 259 poems by deceased Brazilian and Portuguese poets in their distinctive styles (Playfair, 2010). Incidentally, Chico also provided very precise survival evidence which was later verified by researchers (*ibid.*: 85–92).

Given this lack of awareness and disinclination to probe beneath the surface, it is hardly surprising that some of the outstanding *prima facie* evidence for survival is totally unknown outside the narrow confines of the history of psychical research. I think, for example, of the work of Thomas G. Hamilton, a Canadian doctor, a man of strong social conscience and impeccable character who worked with local mediums to produce automatic writing and a substantial number of materialisations (many photographically recorded) suggestive of life after death (Hamilton, T.G., 1947/1972). To my knowledge there has never been the least accusation of fraud associated with his work. There has also been the remarkable body of phenomena collectively gathered under the heading of *The Scole Report*, after the village in Norfolk where most of it took place. It spawned a substantial investigation by the SPR, a more popular book, the publication of a very detailed diary by the leading figure, Robin Foy, and, a good few years later, a DVD (Coleman, 2010). Yet the impact on the wider cultural consciousness has been almost zero. There are issues about the tightness of conditions under which the phenomena manifested at Scole but, at the very least, there is a *prima facie* case for something remarkable having taken place.

Because of this formidable mixture of explicit and tacit hostility to mediumship and the whole field of the paranormal, I decided to prepare myself through as much background reading and research as I could. I have identified from all this eight central lines of enquiry to help me assess the experiences that Anne and I have had with the ten mediums. I would argue that any medium worth her or his salt should be prepared to recognise these issues and help to address them—provided the sitter/investigator is operating in a courteous and respectful fashion. Several of these questions deal with philosophical and metaphysical matters as I gradually began to realise the complexity of the problems involved.

Finally, I have also had to be aware of the limitations of this individual and highly personal enquiry. I was not part of a team investigating mediums under controlled conditions. In fact, when I started my reading and personal research the amount of recent work of this nature in print was exiguous. In 1996 Emily Williams Cook (Kelly) lamented in a conference report

> Regrettably, however, the primary thing that the conference highlighted for me was the distressing state of survival research today.[3]

And it is really only the pioneering and courageous activity of Kelly herself (2010; 2011), Schwartz (2002), Robertson and Roy (2001), Beischel (2007; 2010) — and the useful sceptical responses of Hyman (2003) and O'Keeffe/Wiseman (2005) to some of this research — that has revived interest in this aspect of parapsychology. My knowledge of this body of work came too late to help me devise a formal research strategy for my sittings with mediums but it has helped considerably in the assessment questions I formulated. These are:

1. How accurate was the information the medium provided and how much of it could have been obtained by prior research?

2. What other explanations (apart from the paranormal) could there be for the provision of accurate information?

3. Can a sitter replicate phenomena across a number of mediums and does this support or weaken the survival hypothesis?

---

[3] And despite the work cited, the trend continues. In his otherwise excellent book on ESP, Carpenter (2012) has in its 487 pages just one reference to survival after death (107) and a few brief references to mediums. He acknowledges the pioneering work of Myers in getting us to recognise the importance of unconscious mental functioning and this was obviously an anticipation of Carpenter's 'First Sight' model of psi. Would that he might take a further leaf from Myers' work and focus his attention on *Human Personality and Its Survival of Bodily Death* like his great precursor.

4. *Are there any good examples of high quality historical and contemporary performances by mediums, under acceptable conditions, that would support the survival hypothesis?*

5. *Are there converging lines of evidence from other sources that would support and corroborate the survival hypothesis?*

6. *Given positive results from the above lines of enquiry, does this necessarily mean that the source of the information is a discarnate personality?*

7. *Is it possible to identify those conditions which make for successful sittings and what are the implications of this for the guidance and training of sitters, mediums, and researchers?*

8. *What does evidence from mediumship tell us about the nature and experience of the 'we' that might survive, and are there any lessons we can draw from this as to how we should live our lives here and now?*

1. *How accurate was the information the medium provided and how much of it could have been obtained by prior research?*

One way to assess the accuracy of information is to develop scoring schemes (rather like examiners' marking schemes). As I read the relevant literature, however, I became suspicious of these for they tended to be unnecessarily complex in their attempts to measure levels of accuracy and in their trying to combine the assessing of individual statements with a global figure for general credibility (Schwartz, 2002: 118–19). I, therefore, adopted the simpler method outlined in Part 1. Appendix 1 gives the detail of the mediums' performances. Just the key salient points will be commented on here. Three of the sittings were between 85 and 90% accurate. Four were between 68 and 79%, and three ranged from 38 to 61% accuracy. Six of the mediums produced true statements to the level of 70% accuracy or above. The number of false statements across all the mediums was remarkably low and in two cases no errors were made at all.

A number of the factual statements, though accurate, were on a relatively general level of specificity, and I consider in question 2 whether or not they could have been generated by some standard patter or set of fraudulent techniques. On the other hand, no matter how general, they were apposite and they did fit into the overall narrative of our family lives and personalities. Some of the items were at a high level of specificity, as I mentioned in my assessment comments after each sitting in Part 1. I summarise them here for convenience: the colour of Ralph's bedroom wallpaper (an unusual lilac which we remarked on when we moved in), the name Mrs Bennett who, with my grandmother, babysat him and Daniel and spoilt them rotten with sweet treats, the car park replacing the gardens at the back of their houses, the fact I had six siblings, the 24 chapters in my Myers draft (which I had never counted), the angel lamp which we had taken from our first house and which fascinated Ralph as a child, my love of Chopin and my music teacher Elizabeth (Richards not Roberts — I considered this a reasonable enough approximation to score as true) of whom I had been particularly fond because of the earnest conversations we used to have at the keyboard, and the importance of the dates 22nd November and the 6th July. Also highly specific were the description of Ralph's personality, appearance, and interests, and the character of my father. Ralph came across with great force and vividness in our first sitting, and my sitting with medium 9 was almost overwhelming in the speed and consistency of its portrait of my father. On the other hand, the spraying out of Christian names, in varying degrees, by all of the mediums, was particularly irritating. It all seemed rather cheap and desperate. So these, though factually accurate, were only so in the most banal sense.

The question of predictive statements needs some consideration, and I assess them *en bloc* in Appendix 2. However, there was one puzzling matter (I hesitate to call it a prediction) in the sitting with medium 9 that merits discussion here:

You will have a period of sharp pains in the ears   Pred

Also a whistling sound   Pred
Watch out for it

This happened early one morning in December 2008 (though I had completely forgotten about the 'prediction'). I was half dozing when suddenly there came a whooshing/whistling sound and I distinctly heard the name 'Fred'. The noise was external, or appeared external to me. Myers was called 'Fred' by his friends and this incident occurred just at the time I had received very positive responses from two readers of the draft manuscript of my book. Did I really think the discarnate Myers had managed to communicate his approval? I could only put it down to suggestion and the semi-sleep state I was in, in fact a typical hypnopompic state, a term coined by Myers himself!

There is also the question of how to assess statements which seem to contain a high degree of symbolic content. The statement may be presented in picture form, and as a factual item be impossible to assess. Yet it has great meaning for the individual concerned. Robertson and Roy (2001) give the example of the medium seeing 'a giant wheatsheaf in the middle of a harvested field with a man sitting on top of it and waving'. The sitter's dead husband had been the proprietor of the Wheatsheaf Inn. I had one vivid example of this in the sittings. Medium 9 relayed to me an image transmitted by my father of shards from an archaeological dig being reassembled as vases. This seemed magnificently apposite to me. It fitted exactly with my projected work on the cross-correspondences (which I was hesitating about). The cross-correspondences were a highly intricate set of communications ostensibly transmitted by the discarnate Myers and others to a number of geographically isolated mediums. They were fragmentary (like shards) but when put together made sense (the assembled vase). 'He' couldn't have chosen a better image for the proposed task. It was a very powerful image, emotionally and intuitively, for me, and helped to confirm my provisional decision to do work on that subject.

Another interesting category is factual statements by the discarnate as to what their loved ones are doing now, thus apparently demonstrating a consciousness that has survived death and which continues to interact and empathise with us. In general, I could not find anything particularly persuasive in this category—advice to me not to get too isolated which was certainly relevant but not unique, the coming back to see us in our house (standard Spiritualistic stuff), the lights, the bloody lights (a little more specific), Anne singing round the house, me signing a contract. All much of a muchness. I put them in the factual or other category depending on whether there was any verifiable evidence linked to them. However, one specific item in the sitting with the third medium did move me and give me pause for thought:

Picture of you (Trevor) agitated at a table	True
Tapping on it with a penny, in the registry	True
Waiting for a death certificate	True

I remembered the incident vividly and I have described it in Part 1. What was I doing here? What was this ritual, this pantomime? What did any of this have to do with Ralph? How had I got here? And I tapped a penny over and again on the table and watched my hand, as in a close-up in a film, tapping, tapping, and tapping, and then I stopped. It reminded me of Rossetti's poem of grief and loss, *The Woodspurge*—how sometimes in great distress all one can focus on or all that stands out in one's despair is a specific physical object:

> From perfect grief there need not be
> Wisdom or even memory:
> One thing then learnt remains to me,—
> The woodspurge has a cup of three.

In short, the statements produced were a mixture of the highly specific, general, and the occasionally silly. But was there any way that the more impressive and interesting information could have been gathered by the mediums before we met them? Two sittings were through contacts my sister Carolyn had made: the first and the third. All she had told the mediums was that we had suffered the loss of a son. Nothing was said about age, personality, or life and situation. I had two sittings with medium 2, about a year apart, so it is possible that he recognised me and recycled the same information. All the mediums were complete strangers to us and all, except the first one, were made at relatively short notice leaving little time for background research.

There was scarcely any information about Ralph accessible in the public domain — only one of the mediums lived in the West Country. Most of the information given by the mediums was not of a public nature and the mediums at the CPS and the SAGB in London would only have had my surname as a baseline for further research. Theoretically it could be argued that they might, in cahoots with the receptionists/administrators, have got my credit card details and used these as a starting point for further research. But such ingenuity could surely have been put to greater financial reward than the £35 or £50 fee of the satisfied customer?

However, the situation has changed dramatically since my/our earliest sittings. Any sitter with a medium now needs to check what information is available about them through *Facebook/YouTube* or other social networking channels. This is an area which is bound to impact on the way everyone investigating the paranormal operates, and could make the naïve participant very vulnerable to exploitation. The advice and guidance of Wiseman and Morris on sitting with and the testing of psychic claimants is even more relevant today than at the time of first publication (1995). For example, I have had one sitting since June 2009 (when my Myers book was published) which was with medium 10 in October 2010. Did he Google me? And was that the source of the prediction about my writing books, future journeys, and further projects?

All the mediums appeared genuine to me and I, in fact, liked all of them. However, fraud seems to be an inescapable part of this field (whether in individual sessions or public performances) and one has to be alive to it. From my background reading I knew of the distressing and confusing incidents in recent years where mediums with outstanding national reputations like Doris Stokes (Wilson, 1987: 74-9) and Gordon Higginson (Paul, 2010) had been accused of using 'normal' means to gain information about their audiences—either by getting it from pre-show confederates in the audience or by giving free tickets to people who had sat with them before, or by accessing names and addresses from other sources. I should stress that in those cases the charges have been strongly rebutted and that many people in the Spiritualist movement hold the above individuals in very high regard.

There are even more outrageous examples. M. Lamar Keene (1976), in *The Psychic Mafia,* described how he and his colleagues eavesdropped on people by the use of an 'electronic sound collector'. By this and other methods he shared a network of information that reached across the United States. William Roy was an equally skilled rogue who operated in England (with judicious periods abroad to avoid problems) who used similar techniques. Visitors to his 'Hampstead Psychic Centre' had to leave all belongings in the cloakroom (they were rifled through for anything useful) and microphones were hidden in the waiting room (Price *et al.*, 2011: 138). And this is not just an historical phenomenon. For example, in 2001, George Dobinson, in *The Paranormal Review* (2001: 10), reported that in France the estimated turnover from telephone readings and visits to mediums was 20 billion francs. He also mentioned that Magistrates' courts in various parts of France had been cracking down on fraudulent mediums and deliberately misleading advertisements.

One final point. It is often argued that mediums ought to produce high quality and meaningful statements rather than the trivial material they often do. In fact the great Thomas Huxley made that point when invited to a séance in the late 19th century. He did not want to listen to the gossip of a washer woman or a crossing sweeper. However, an equally great man, the psychologist William James, has put the counter argument. As James Hyslop (1919: 247), himself a tireless investigator of psychic phenomena, wrote

> In the investigation of psychic phenomena no one ever insisted more rigidly than he that personal identity is the fundamental problem and that only the remotest trivial facts would prove that identity.

In James's case, after his own death, these facts, communicated by the medium Mrs Chenoweth, included a precise description of his largely vegetarian diet in the last few years of his life (*ibid.*: 238). The acid test is, in such situations, to distinguish the precisely trivial from the commonplace trivial. In Ralph's case, most people would remember objects from childhood that fascinated them, but for how many would it be an external house light shaped in the form of a winged angel or fairy?

2. *What other explanations (apart from the paranormal) could there be for the provision of accurate information?*

Given then that it was not possible for the mediums to have acquired the information beforehand, what might they have gleaned from us at the sittings? I was very careful in my behaviour at each sitting, as was Anne in the ones she attended, to say as little as possible consistent with maintaining a positive and civilised atmosphere. Listening and re-listening to the tapes I could not find any significant leakages. But a couple of incidents made me pause. The medium I sat with twice was given no information at all by me except on the first occasion when I said that I had hoped to contact my son. He then gave me a correct description of Ralph and his circumstances but I had furnished the prompt. I also noticed a couple of occasions over the ten sittings where it might be said that I provided some clues: as in the reading with the star CPS medium, when he asked me a leading question:

Tell me, Trevor, what do you want to do when you grow up?

This is worth expanding on. He was a charming man with a certain wit and style, and he had given sittings for many celebrities. He spoke rapidly, often accurately, and generally without fishing. I got the distinct feeling that this question occurred when he was flagging or when the 'energy' was fading. I gave him (which I certainly should not have done) the information that I wrote and wanted to continue writing. He had, however, before this made the statement that I was involved in communications and writing, and he had already given me much accurate information, so I intuitively felt it might be useful to support him. It just seemed to give him a boost and also led to further very relevant comments. It might well be the case that even genuine mediums have to busk a bit and develop strategies to keep going when the 'connection' fades.

That was why I generally found it best not to interrupt the flow or to adopt a negative or hostile attitude which might have destroyed the atmosphere. An examination of the tape afterwards quite often clarified matters that didn't make sense at the time. Some researchers suggest that the sitter should remain silent at all times or get a friend to take a sitting for them, or be hidden behind a screen. In fact, one would hope that professional researchers would want to create a variety of controlled or semi controlled situations in order to establish the best fit between tightness of control and quality of performance and the amount and degree of interaction between medium and sitter. There is very little research evidence on this, given the traditional emphasis on proving survival (or not) rather than the process (the non-sensory channels by which the medium accessed information and the most conducive environment).

However, my concern over the involuntary leakage of information led me to explore in some detail the techniques of cold reading, including the classic book on the subject by Ian Rowland (2002). I do not completely agree with Rowland's position or his analysis, but the book gives a very clear idea of what to look out for and the kind of criteria to use when judging mediumistic statements. It gave me considerable pause for thought that some of the statements that I found particularly moving had the same level of generality that Rowland gave as examples of cold reading in his book. For me, the key insight of Rowland's book was that the sitters did much of the work in generating the meaning and validating the authenticity of the session. They created their own little local miracle from generalised statements and scenarios based on the class and age of the sitter, plus some simple specific statements based on common probabilities. It was the verbal equivalent of spotting an angel or the Virgin Mary in a rock formation or the clouds.

I applied this to my own readings and one item stood out: my father apologising for being too harsh and critical. It was clear to me that a man in his late sixties in England would often have had a father who spent time in the services and who would have held the traditional view of masculinity of the men of his generation. It was certainly, for the fraudulent medium, a script worth trying. I am not saying that this perception completely invalidated that sitting. It did, however, mean that I had to look very carefully at it to see what other supporting evidence there was — either way. And that sitting, of them all, with medium 9, was the one in which I was nearest to tears

You felt isolated at school and he did not understand	True
He saw sensitivity as a weakness not a strength	True
He apologises	Other
He was too harsh and unforgiving	True

What was additionally alarming was that medium 10 used almost identical language in describing my relationship with my father, thus reinforcing my suspicion that cold reading was being deployed.

Furthermore, the cold reading technique can be powerfully enhanced by the charisma of the medium and by the artificial situation the sitters find themselves in. Schouten (1994) has written effectively on these points. It often occurred to me over these years that visiting a medium was, in some ways, not that different from going to the dentist, having your haircut, seeing a doctor. I was putting myself in the hands of somebody with expertise which I hadn't got and who would be concentrating exclusively on me for a fixed period of time. The instinctive tendency to trust the experts and to accept their statements and their authority is quite natural, and under the influence of powerful emotions and possible subtle manipulation by an individual of a certain charm, it is not easy to remain objective.

It also forcibly struck me, both during the preliminary research reading and at the sitting, and listening to the transcripts afterwards, that Anne and I could not always escape the subjective nature of our assessments. This is a difficult problem to surmount (O'Keeffe and Wiseman, 2005). We had plenty of true/false statements—quite impressive the number of true ones at first sight. But I/we needed to distinguish between different kinds of true statements. What was the evidence base for each statement, where was it, how objective was it, and to what extent was it highly specific to us and to Ralph? (See Appendix 1: 164.)

I came across the research of Robertson and Roy (2001)[4] which provided some reassurance on this point. They did a considerable amount of work with mediums to test the premise that much of the material they generated was so vague and broad that it could apply to almost anyone. Their work seemed to demonstrate that the best performers produced accurate statements which were picked out by the intended recipient and not by other sitters in the control groups.

But there was one final question—could all these statements have been the product of lucky guesswork built upon a foundation of sophisticated cold reading? Were there any

---

[4] They later demonstrated under double and triple blind conditions (2001; 2004) that mediums could provide accurate and specific information. There has been some criticism of their approach and their statistics (Kelly, 2011) but this does not totally invalidate their conclusions.

statistical tools for evaluating probabilities in this area? Was I hugely exaggerating the impressiveness of some of the information put forward? There were two questions I really wished to have answered. The first was—even though individual statements might not be remarkable—was their particular combination with a large number of other accurate statements well above what chance would suggest? I began to realise how difficult this was when I read an article (Rogers, Davis and Fisk, 2009) which examined the hypothesis that believers in the paranormal were more inclined to make conjunction errors in reasoning than non-believers. That is, they were more likely to 'misperceive co-occurring (conjunct) events as being more likely than singular (constituent) events alone'. I was also put on my guard by an article of Susan Blackmore's (1997) which listed the kind of statements suggestive of the paranormal (but really naturally occurring) which people had a tendency to believe in. The article, in fact, showed that there was no difference between believers and non-believers in the paranormal with regard to their general estimation of probabilities, but her research (6238 replies from a questionnaire in the *Daily Telegraph*) did demonstrate that statements one might find quite convincing in a reading could be claimed by a fair section of the population:

> There is someone called Jack in my family 21.3%
> I am one of three children 26.4%
> I have a scar on my left knee 33.5%

Therefore, the second question I was interested in was posed by the early psychical researchers Saltmarsh and Soal (1930–31) of each individual statement the medium made—is the statement correct and for what part of the population does the statement hold? To some extent I could answer the first, guarding against the subjectivity of the judgment already mentioned. But the second issue seemed to be intractable for somebody conducting an individual and highly personal investigation. Two early investigators in the history of psychical research, Thomas and Hyslop, each at different times (Schouten, 1994) tried to create a population or a reference class against which the statements from the sittings with mediums could be assessed. But these populations were constructed artificially post hoc after the sittings. I did not have the resources to do this regardless of any statistical arguments for or against it.

In my early enthusiasm to answer the first question I had originally started to calculate the conditional probabilities (following Schwartz, 2002) of my most impressive specific statements. Surely the odds against someone specifying the precise number of chapters in a book (say 1 in 30), a specific birthday (1 in 365), a significant day (1 in 365), and so on, would be enormous? Yet I quickly became aware that though these certainly were concrete items and not susceptible to subjective bias, they were few and far between. They were also embedded in material that was not statistically independent. As Hacking (2009: 41) states

> Two events are independent when the occurrence of one does not influence the probability of the occurrence of the other.

Looking back over the tapes and transcripts I could clearly see how many of the statements were linked with each other and how different the reference groups were from which statements were derived. Some could be seen as straightforward odds calculations like the drawing of cards from a pack, while others (personal physical characteristics, life events, memories, beliefs, attitudes) had no such easily identifiable set of circumstances or population from which they were drawn. I had, reluctantly, to rely on other sources of authority and justification. It should be noted that there are ways round this problem which deserve future amplification (Schouten, 1994; O'Keefe and Wiseman, 2005) but considerable resources and thought need to be put into it before it could be set up for the individual sitter.

If conventional statistical analysis would not work, I wondered if a Bayesian approach might not be applicable. For Thomas Bayes (an eighteenth-century clergyman) had developed a formula for calculating probability based on individual degrees of belief, and I had read there was considerable discussion as to whether Bayes' approach could be formally applied in legal situations. Moreover, the judging of evidence in legal and historical situations seemed to me rather like analysing and assessing the statements that mediums made, particularly in relation to personal identity. However, I found that the application of Bayesian statistics to the legal field was rather contentious (Hodgson, 1995) because of the subjective nature of the estimate of prior probabilities and the difficulties of establishing an agreed numerical value for each item of evidence. The same would clearly apply when assessing the statements of mediums. It seemed to me, therefore, that until there was some wide professional consensus on these issues, it was wiser to present the material as it stood.

3. Can a sitter replicate phenomena across a number of mediums and does this support or weaken the survival hypothesis?

Replicability is not always easy even in mainstream science let alone the more opaque and shifting world of psychical research or parapsychology (Collins, 1992: 29–33). One must, therefore, apply the test of replication sensitively to the performance of mediums—a field whose conditions we know little of, individuals we may never have met in our lives before and whose environment may change in subtle ways from day to day, and whose interaction with us may well affect the quality of the information received: even leaving out other variables from the geomagnetic (Powell, 2009) to the nature and difficulties of the process of communication with the putative discarnate! Kaplan (1998: 127–8) has strongly stressed this point in the wider context of the behavioural and social sciences generally.

On the other hand, though my/our sittings were in no sense laboratory experiments or held under tight conditions, they did take place under relatively standard circumstances

—a sitting with a medium who did not know the sitter(s), from another part of the UK, and to whom I/we responded in a fairly limited and guarded way. So the question is, in these similar contexts, did anything evidential emerge across the readings to suggest that the 'same' discarnate personalities were communicating?

There was a fair degree of consistency across most of the sessions. Ralph appeared in eight of the readings and in seven of them the general nature of his passing described—a sudden death caused by some form of accident. There was an inconsistency here. Once the death was stated as caused by his error—*I paid the price*. On another occasion he said that it was not his fault. It is possible to reconcile these contradictions by interpreting the statement *not my fault* as an indication that he had not deliberately committed suicide. But I accept that this is unsatisfactory.

His character and personality was quite vividly and accurately described: his cheekiness, his popularity, his sensitivity, his love of water sports, of travel, his fondness for monkeys, his semi-professional success in music, his career and situation at the time of his death. My father also appeared frequently and vividly (in eight of the ten sessions) and was very accurately delineated: his smart appearance, his belief in discipline, his rather abrasive nature, and the way he kept people, including his children, at a distance. My maternal grandmother was also mentioned and her role in my life clearly stated. These in fact would be (plus my maternal grandfather who appeared more faintly twice) the very people that I would want to come through. It is noticeable that in the three sittings Anne and I shared the main focus was on Ralph with only very minimal glancing references to other personalities. Anne and my father did not get on—new woman vs. traditional man—and it made sense that he would come through most strongly in individual sittings with me.

It was remarkable, too, that across the sittings consistent statements about me were made. I ignore the commonplace points about self-doubt and needing more self-confidence, which applies to virtually the whole human race, but just mention here the emphasis on new challenges, on being busier than ever when well into formal retirement, the writing and publishing of books, and the constant mental activity: all of which points were and are true. At least two of the mediums mentioned that I had mediumistic/healing potential. Again, I discounted this, since it seemed the kind of stock flattery to which a dubious medium or psychic might resort. On the other hand, one medium said it ran in my family, and, as I wrote earlier, two of my sisters had become Reiki healers, and the third said that she had occasionally been troubled by odd phenomena. I, too, had had precognitive dreams and premonitions. Maybe there was some capacity there in me. Maybe. Maybe not.

My experience of the replication of similar statements across a number of mediums is small-scale compared to the results of the dedicated and systematic research of J.F. Thomas in the 1920s and 1930s. Thomas (1937) was a senior school administrator in the United States: a quiet, perceptive, and highly methodical man. He held, directly or through proxies, hundreds of sittings in America and England with leading mediums, and he took great care to verify the evidence provided, hiring a graduate student to work the whole of one summer with him to seek out objective evidence in diaries, physical objects, and other records. Thomas called the process of replication 'amplification', stressing the way the same topic was taken up by a number of mediums with both similar and additional statements being made. The main communicator at these sittings was his wife who, again, by consistently identifying herself in a characteristic manner, provided a further, impressive example of replication.

4. Are there any good examples of high quality historical and contemporary performances by mediums, under acceptable conditions, that would support the survival hypothesis?

The scientific community (with a few honourable exceptions) has displayed a cavalier ignorance of the best evidence[5] for survival, both historical and contemporary. On the other side of the coin, the Spiritualist community and many individual mediums have been guarded and suspicious at the thought of formal assessment and testing. The division is a most unfortunate one and I will give some examples from the Spiritualist literature as they tend to be less well known and discussed in academic circles. I cannot see how anyone reading the accounts of the mediumship of John Sloan or Albert Best—both from Glasgow, the one before the second world war and the one after—can fail to appreciate that something really significant is going on. Incidentally, both were men, which gives the lie to the offensive remark still sometimes peddled that mediums are just self-deceiving and dotty women or, in its more subtly patronising form, that it requires a feminine sensitivity to make contact with the dead.

Arthur Findlay was a Scottish stockbroker who investigated and publicised Sloan's mediumship. Sloan so impressed Findlay that he bequeathed his country house, Stansted, to the Spiritualist movement as a residential and training centre. Sloan was a quiet and unassuming working man who, when in trance, would generate voices external to his vocal chords, which seemed to provide excellent evidence for life after death. As Findlay stated (1932: 55–56): 'In the medium's presence, but quite apart from him, voices, claiming to be those of deceased people, speak, and when

---

[5] Three of the most impressive mediums in the Anglo-Saxon world were Leonora Piper (1857–1950), Gladys Osborne Leonard, and Eileen Garrett (1892–1970). Each of them cooperated fully with investigators and, despite robust criticism, for many, their work stands up (Angoff, 2009; Smith, 1964; Gauld, 1982).

replied to answer back intelligently, showing that there is not only a mind behind the voice but that the intelligence is able to hear as well speak.' Naturally, Findlay was highly suspicious at first. He thought of accomplices, 'a regular system of gathering information', and the complete physical impossibility of the buried dead speaking. So, for him, the initial balance of probabilities was strongly in favour of fraud, even though Sloan sat in the darkness for more than three hours and 'Thirty separate voices spoke that night, of different tone and accent, they gave their names, their correct earth addresses and spoke to the right people, were recognised, and referred to intimate family matters'. Furthermore, later on that same evening his father and another individual spoke to him of a private matter which he, Findlay, alone knew about. He had not given his name and he was a stranger to everyone in the room. Sloan also refused payment which further impressed Findlay. So began the start of his detailed investigation.

In all (based on notes of thirty-nine sittings with Sloan) 280 separate communications were given to Findlay or friends he brought with him. He classed 180 of them A1 as 'it was impossible for the medium or any other person present to have known about them', and 100 as A2 since the information was theoretically in the public domain. In both types of cases the amount of factual inaccuracy was miniscule (*ibid.*: 92–106). To give one example, Findlay brought his brother to a sitting. He was not introduced. No one knew he had been in the army, that he had been stationed part of the time at Kessingland near Lowestoft, and that he had been training gunners. An Eric Saunders, whom the brother did not recognise or remember, came through and, despite trick questions from the brother, gave him a string of accurate information about himself and their time at Kessingland. He said that he was present that evening because Findlay's brother had once done him a good turn during training and just before he had gone to France in August 1917. The brother vaguely thought the favour might have been obtaining leave for the man. He was able later to confirm that an Eric Saunders (through the pocket diary of the brother's old corporal) had been trained by him and departed to France at the time stated. The case appears fraud proof and difficult to explain by telepathy.

The second body of evidence comes from David Kennedy's fine book (1974) about communication with his wife Ann after her death, largely but not exclusively through the mediumship of Albert Best. Kennedy and his wife had a lifelong interest in psychical research and had read widely in the literature of the SPR. Kennedy, a Church of Scotland minister, was astonished to find how few of his fellow clergy knew anything about this material or had reflected in any analytical way on life after death. He had twelve sittings with mediums in the months after Ann's death. These were all banal messages of general comfort, though in each case the medium stated that the communicators were his wife and his mother (*ibid.*: 107). However, much more substantial evidence came from Albert Best who would often telephone unprompted with information from Kennedy's wife, clearly indicating that she knew of his current thoughts and actions (*ibid.*: 103–5). On one occasion Best said that his wife was aware that he was still reading the book he had been looking at earlier and that if he turned to page 55 he would find the name of a common friend. He did and there was the name. The book Kennedy was reading was a rare one and completely unknown to Best. Sometime later Kennedy was desperately looking for clean clerical collars (he had a funeral service in an hour's time). At that moment Best rang up and said that Ann was telling him where the clean collars were. They were found where she said. He then asserted that she was urging Kennedy get the soiled collars clean and that there were twenty-three of them. And there were. Kennedy kept Albert Best at a distance for obvious reasons and much of their contact was by telephone. It can of course be argued that we have only Kennedy's word for the nature of their relationship and the events that took place, and that he was deranged by grief. The best counter to this is to read his book. He comes across as a highly intelligent, well read, humane, and balanced individual.

A collection of some of the most impressive examples of Albert Best's healing and mediumship powers are contained in *'Best' of Both Worlds* (Cattanach, 2007, with a foreword by Professor Archie Roy). I doubt if many parapsychologists have ever read or even considered reading something that they would dismiss as highly anecdotal or Spiritualistic, but anyone who looks through it with an open mind can surely see the genuineness of the man and the remarkable nature of his gifts: there are some outstanding examples in the book (23–25, 38, 40–44) which demonstrate a precision light years beyond those any cold reader could manage. I shall just, here, expand on one of these references since the evidence provided was not consciously known by the recipient and required further research for its verification. Ken King and his wife Joan attended a church demonstration by Albert Best in Scotland in 1977. Best said that he had a message for them from a Henry Montgomery who had lived at 77a Park Street, Abbotsford (a suburb of Melbourne), and who had known Ken King's parents. Extensive research (the houses in that number range had been demolished to make way for new buildings) eventually revealed that a Hy.A. Montgomery had lived at 77a Park Street during the years when Ken King's parents were living close by.

If the comment is that these mediums were never tested by competent scientists, firstly one can say that neither Findlay nor Kennedy were gullible individuals and both held down demanding jobs that gave them ample experience of the world and its ways. Findlay was a stockbroker and Kennedy had been an electronic engineer and consultant before he trained for the ministry. Secondly, neither Sloan nor Best were out to make money from mediumship. They were modest and retiring individuals who put comfort and support for the bereaved beyond any external validation of their credentials. Thirdly, it was, and probably still is, rare to find a scientist with the right combination of qualities to work with such mediums. I shall consider this issue in more detail in a later section.

In case the objection is that these are just two incredibly rare and bizarre examples, I would refer the reader to recent books by Tymn (2008; 2011a) and by Fontana (2005), which between them cover many high quality historical and contemporary examples of evidence for survival. However, probably the most immediately accessible source of good case studies is the Association for Evaluation and Communication of Evidence for Survival (AECES) website. The team responsible for this site post only those cases that meet their demanding evidential criteria. The criteria (slightly adapted and summarised by me) are:

- Cases that are over-complicated, redolent of deception, make outlandish claims in terms of past lives or alien inspiration, have offensive elements in them, or seem to promote a specific agenda are, *prima facie*, ruled out.
- There are two essential criteria: how likely is it that the source is discarnate? The likelihood increases with the ruling out of alternative explanations. The second criterion: how reliable is the report, the testimony? Both these elements can be scored — the first up to 200 and the second up to 100.
- The alternatives that have to be ruled out (as far as is humanly possible) with reference to the first criterion are: the accessing of the conscious mind of individuals involved in the activity, the accessing of the unconscious mind of individuals involved in the activity, the accessing of the conscious and unconscious minds of individuals not involved in the activity, the accessing of information from existing objects and documents, and the accessing of information from specific events that have been registered in some way in some kind of cosmic data base.
- The second criterion emphasises the reliability and quality of the evidence rather than its original source.

> Is there more than one testimony available? Are the witnesses trained and experienced in the gathering and assessing of evidence? Are there audio/video tapes (and/or transcripts of these) available for public assessment? How many sitters sat with how many mediums, and how complementary and consistent was the information produced?
> - AECES also stress that OBEs, and presumably NDEs (see glossary), while suggestive of the existence of a mental world, do not, in themselves, constitute the highest quality evidence for life after death and should only be seen, as I see them, as supportive evidence.
> - A decision-making tree, based largely on yes/no questions, allows the cases to be scored and only those that achieve 250 out of 300 are put in the survival top 40.

I would recommend that anyone who (a) believes there is no evidence of any quality for survival, and (b) that only the simple-minded and emotional accept what does exist as convincing should access some of these cases and work through the scoring themselves.

One caveat. The ranking order of the top forty changes as new cases or fresh evidence comes in. This is important. Even some of the very best cases may not be what they seem and may be vulnerable to the discovery of later evidence. A couple of examples will suffice, though neither of these is in the AECES top forty. In David Fontana's survey of evidence for the afterlife, the Chaffin Case is accorded high status (Fontana, 2005: 52–53). This is an apparent after death communication rather than one received at a formal sitting with a medium, but the issue of possible later discreditation remains the same. In June 1925, in North Carolina, the deceased father of James P. Chaffin allegedly appeared at his bedside stating that his will was in his overcoat pocket. A note was found in the coat which led the relatives to the family bible in which the actual will was concealed. This will divided his estate equally between the four children. A previous will had given the estate to Chaffin's 3rd son and he contested the validity of the later will. However, two neighbours testified and ten witnesses in court stated that the handwriting was that of Chaffin's father. Fontana discusses the obvious possibility of fraud but rules it out, ultimately, in favour of the survivalist hypothesis. However, Mary Roach (2005: 241-59), almost eighty years later, revisited the case, interviewed surviving family members, and hired a forensic handwriting expert who cast doubt on the authenticity of the father's signature on the later will. The likelihood now increases that the members of the family excluded in the first will colluded to fake both ghost and second will in order to redress the obvious injustice.

Secondly, Playfair and Keen published, in 2004, a case that they believed was strongly suggestive of survival. This was the remarkable story of the apparent return of a murdered woman from beyond the grave to the medium Christine Holohan so that her unknown murderer could be caught. 'Accurate, detailed and specific information' was provided (Playfair and Keen, 2004: 1), and it is argued that this gave the police sufficient evidence and impetus to solve the case. However, there have been strong criticisms (e.g. Youens, 2006), suggesting that much of her information could have come from normal sources and that advances in forensic science rather than the medium's input was what really brought the murderer to justice. As well as the conflicting interpretations, the case is also rendered complex by its sensational nature and the attitude of the police and the press to the involvement of psychics in unsolved cases. The best examination of the interplay of forces at work in those situations where mediums aid the police is Lyons' and Truzzi's (1991) *The Blue Sense*. Such cases may, at root, be very powerful ones in favour of survival after death, particularly in the sense of an individual personality demonstrating purpose, motivation, and intent (as opposed to the fragmented and disconnected nature of some mediumistic communication), but they need to be examined with care and caution.

Well-known to students of psychical research, but forgotten for many years and only recently revived, are proxy sittings (sittings on behalf of someone else with carefully controlled or no information provided to the medium). Particularly impressive are the sessions which Nea Walker (1927; 1935) and Drayton Thomas (Smith, S., 1964) conducted on behalf of the grieving. There was also the extensive series of proxy sittings held for the American researcher J.T. Thomas, mentioned above. In addition, one particularly impressive proxy sitting in which E.R. Dodds was involved should be noted, since Dodds was a determined and highly intelligent sceptic. He asked (on behalf of W.S. Lewis) Drayton Thomas to get Mrs Leonard to contact Frederic Macaulay who was Lewis's father-in-law. She provided 124 pieces of information of which 95 were fair or above, 24 were poor or doubtful, and 5 were wrong. Dodds (1977: 107–8) concluded that either it was a case of survival or very powerful telepathy. He inclined to the latter. In more recent years, Emily Kelly (2011) has revived this technique and argued for its value as a research tool, and it has also been taken up in different forms by Schwartz and Beischel.

One very interesting category of cases is those where an individual gatecrashes or drops in on another's sitting.[6] For example, having written the biography of Myers, one such account that interested me was that of Hunt (1936: 162–63), who attended a direct voice sitting with Mrs Estelle Roberts:

> I received in complete darkness a kindly message of appreciation and thanks, voiced in the most cultured accents, and professedly on behalf of a group, from one who claimed to be F W H Myers... I am convinced that none of the living persons in the room... could have given utterance

---

[6] I had one indirect experience of this nature. One of Anne's friends (see page 41) sat with a medium in Manchester and Ralph appeared to come through, though not expected or sought by her.

to the beautifully-phrased sentiments and educated diction of the words I heard addressed to me.

Of course, since the drop-in is unexpected it may easily be the product of conscious or unconscious fraud on the part of the medium. Only the quality and nature of the evidence will indicate the likely source (Irwin and Watt, 2007: 139–40). Gauld (1982) has provided some impressive examples in this category. An additional problem with drop-in communicators, a term coined by Ian Stevenson, is that they may well be ordinary folk for whom documentary evidence of identity may not easily be obtainable. However, in both the case of these and of proxy sittings (see above) where the information provided can be verified and proven to have been scattered across a variety of sources, rather than in the mind of just one living individual, the evidence for survival, though not completely persuasive, is increasingly powerful.

And there continue to be, up to the present time, cases where mediums provide precise and highly characteristic information about individuals, even if insulated from them by proxy sitter, geography, or time. For example, in 2006 (Eisenbeiss and Hassler, 2006) the *Journal of the Society for Psychical Research* published an account of a chess match, over a substantial period of time, between two Grandmasters, one living (Korchnoi) and one deceased (Maroczy). This was via the automatic writing of the medium Robert Rollans. Through Rollans (who initially knew nothing about chess) a very high level of chess skill was demonstrated, as was a knowledge of chess history and Maroczy's life that it would have been almost impossible to research and acquire. It is true, however, that the conditions of control were not absolutely perfect, but it is, on the face of it, a truly remarkable case and deserves more than the deafening silence it has received in the wider academic community.

Building on the experiments of Schwartz and Robertson and Roy mentioned above, Julie Beischel and her colleagues have significantly contributed to mediumship research in recent years by testing mediums under tightly controlled conditions. The protocol that they had evolved by 2007 meant that they had created an environment in which neither sitter, medium, nor the experimenters involved knew the target for the information that was being generated. This has led to Beischel stating without equivocation that some mediums can report precise and accurate information about the deceased, accessed through other than the normal sensory channels. That appears to be good news but one would like to see it replicated by multi-centre research using the same protocols.

5. Are there converging lines of evidence from other sources that would support and corroborate the survival hypothesis?

Myers, himself, thought that the most systematic approach[7] to the problem was not just to examine actual cases of claimed survival, but also to look at the vast body of evidence that suggested that consciousness was not, in life, totally dependent on the brain, and could both detach itself from the body and influence it—rather than being the passive recipient of the body's forces and energies (Myers, 1904, vol. 1). There is a whole range of phenomena, beyond mediumship, supportive of the statement that mind is not reducible to brain and body but is at times independent of them, which might indicate some form of capacity for continuance after death (Kelly et al., 2007).[8]

These phenomena cover a wide variety of categories: near death and out of body experiences; reincarnation, both naturally occurring and through induced hypnotic regression; death bed visions; after death spontaneous communications; the accounts of individual shamans, healers, and

---

[7] I have not considered mystical experiences, for obvious reasons, as a line of evidence for survival. However, this matter is discussed in great detail by Kelly (E.F.) and Grosso in Kelly, E.F., et al. (2007: 495–575).

[8] Neuroscientist Mario Beauregard reviewing this and other research, including his own (2012: 213), concludes that the model emerging from this research 'suggests that mental functions and personality can survive physical death'.

sensitives; the growing field of instrumental transcommunication (ITC); the well documented poltergeist phenomenon; the development of non-mediumistic techniques for contacting the dead by Moody and by Botkin (the former using a variant of crystal gazing called the psychomanteum, and the latter using structured eye movements); and finally, controlled research into mind-to-mind and mind-to-environment communication and impact, other than through the physical senses.

There has been a substantial increase in near death research in recent years and also in public interest in the topic. But it should be noted that OBE/NDE cases are not a mere copycat New Age fashion. They have been around a long time, were recorded by Myers, and were well-known by the 1930s in Spiritualist circles (Hunt, 1936: 33–52). However, although this work has had implications relevant to the question of the survival of human personality after death (see Kelly, *et al.*, 2007; Cook *et al.*, 1998), there is still limited evidence for the crucial claim. The individual may seem to be experiencing a highly lucid and vivid separation which changes her/his attitude towards death and often their ethical orientation, but what hard evidence is there that their consciousness has actually separated from their body? Cook *et al.* identify three features which individually, but more strongly collectively, are suggestive of survival after death. These are: greater mental clarity at a time when the body is considerably diminished physically; perceiving one's physical body and environment from a perspective distinct from the physical body; and accessing unknown information which, even had they been conscious, was not within the range of their sensory perception (*ibid.*: 381).

Mobbs and Watt (2011) have launched a trenchant attack on such interpretations of the NDE, suggesting physiological reasons for the main phenomena: the awareness of being dead (Cotard syndrome); out of body experiences (sleep paralysis, the stimulation of the right temporoparietal junction); the tunnel of light (visual activity during retinal ischemia when the blood and oxygen supply to the eye lessens, glaucoma); meeting deceased people (hallucinations arising from abnormal dopamine functioning, macular degeneration); euphoric emotions and an acceptance of death (the dopamine and opioid systems operating during a time of traumatic stress). They are, of course, right that these explanatory hypotheses should be thoroughly tested, but there is little if any reference in their paper to challenges to these views. Research more favourable to the 'spiritual' interpretation of the Near Death Experience is severely underrepresented in the references; and in particular there is no mention of the work of Greyson, Ed Kelly and Emily Kelly which addresses in some detail reasons why current physiological explanations of the Near Death Experience are inadequate and unpersuasive (in Holden *et al.*, 2009: 213-34).

Moreover, as Ed Kelly (2011) points out, these kinds of attacks to some extent miss the point. The crucial thing is to get, through controlled studies, the unambiguous establishment of veridical perception when both loss of consciousness and the limitations of the immediate environment would make it impossible under normal conditions. Janice Miner Holden (2009: 185-211) is an NDE researcher who has made this issue a major focus of her research. Holden carried out a literature search and found 107 examples of spontaneous NDEs which provided evidence, of varying strengths, of veridical perception during the NDE experience. A considerable number of these experiences involved 'complete accuracy of perception that the authors corroborated through objective means'. However, none of the five controlled studies she reviews has actually captured a veridical NDE perception. In fact, I would be surprised (though they must continue) if such experiments ever will. In the intense, partly traumatic, partly transcendent nature of an NDE experience, one very much doubts if the consciousness undergoing those experiences has either the 'time or inclination' to focus on artificially deployed pieces of evidence.

Anthony Peake (2011) has written stimulatingly, if speculatively (see Poynton, 2012) on Near Death and Out of Body Experiences (2011). He has argued strongly that we will never get the kind of veridicality hoped for in the above paragraph because all the events and processes are taking place within inner rather than physical space. He argues that it is impossible through this approach to match up observations made in out of body/NDE states with the naturalistic world, since we are not travelling to or observing that world, but rather an interior world of inner space which may partly mirror aspects of the 'real world' but is infinitely much more complex and variable. This theory seems to echo some aspects of traditional esoteric knowledge and its emphasis on the shadowy deceptive world of the astral through which the intrepid occultist must navigate with care. However, this does not mean that there is no relationship between inner and outer space and that the continued effort to search for veridical perception is therefore in vain.

The field of reincarnation research, at first sight, appears to have generated particularly strong evidence for the ability of mind to survive the demise of each individual body as it moves through the centuries and millennia. In fact, a number of philosophers have largely based their belief in life after death on this.[9] There are several sources of evidence. One is the gradual and growing belief of an individual, through dreams, flashbacks, intuitions (often supplemented by their own research), that they have lived before (for example, the case of Arthur Peacock; see Rivas, 1991–2). One of the most romantic UK cases of recent years was the ostensible reincarnation of 13th century Cathars in rural Somerset in the 20th century, as recorded by Arthur Guirdham (1974, etc.) in several books. Harris (2000), however, has cast doubt on the authenticity of these episodes and experiences.

---

[9] For example, Becker (1993). He explicitly states that he will not consider evidence from mediumship. This reflects the low status and level of interest in mediumship research twenty years ago.

A more substantial body of evidence comes from systematic hypnotic age-regression where an individual is taken back beyond birth to a previous existence, sometimes purely out of experimental interest and sometimes for psychotherapeutic reasons. There are a number of published, critically assessed examples of these and even some cases where groups of people seem to have been reincarnated at the same time and place. However, they are difficult to judge fairly given what we know about the capacity of the human mind for cryptomnesia and the dramatising power of the subconscious. There is, too, the negative swirl of claim and counterclaim that washes around famous cases, like those of Bridie Murphy and Jenny Cockill, which makes it difficult to judge them accurately. See Fontana (2005: 426–42) for a good general discussion of these issues.

The several decades of intense and painstaking research of Ian Stevenson must be treated with great respect and consideration. Stevenson, using the forensic and historical methods established by the original leaders of the SPR, has searched for detailed corroborative evidence from witnesses for the statements that children make about their alleged past lives. He has also furnished a number of examples where children have displayed physical marks very closely linked to the injuries that killed them in a previous life. This could be interpreted as very persuasive evidence that the individual consciousness is not tied to the physiological structure of one body and can assume another spatio-temporal track. His work has been criticised on obvious grounds—that the evidence is too old and contaminated by either financial greed or wishful thinking, that it is coloured by different cultural contexts and the need to rely on interpreters. However, Stevenson was fully aware of these factors, and the most recent re-investigation into one of his canonical cases has come down in favour of its authenticity (Mills and Dhiman, 2011). The sceptical point (Smith, J.C., 2010: 242), that the examination of birthmarks and features is purely a question of wishful thinking or pareidolia, seems to me substantially though perhaps not completely rebutted by an examination of the photographs in Stevenson's (1997) *Where Reincarnation and Biology Intersect*. In addition, Moreman (2010: 234), while emphasising the need for caution and the provisional nature of much of the evidence, has pointed out that dismissing reincarnation on *a priori* grounds as fantastic is not an acceptable argument and only a critique based on examining cases in detail is worth consideration.

And, finally, one should stress that such cases are not confined to the Indian subcontinent or parts of Lebanon where the culture encourages the expectation of reincarnation. Stevenson (2003) published an account of European cases of apparent reincarnation to explore that issue and, even more recently, there has been the Leininger (2009) case in America where the parents of a young boy, after very extensive research, believed him to be the reincarnation of a US pilot who was killed fighting the Japanese. All this was against the background of the father's very powerful reluctance (because of his training and his religious beliefs) to take the concept seriously. However, with all such cases, it is impossible to discount the intra-family dynamics, and the language used in the published book is over-egged and predisposes one to scepticism, which is a shame. Cases of apparent possession and obsession also suggest in certain very rare cases a complex and speculative relationship between several minds and one body, and are possible alternative explanations for ostensible reincarnation cases, but I do not have the space to consider them here.

The area of death bed visions, pioneered by Sir William Barrett, has been researched in recent years by Osis and Haraldsson (1997) and by the Fenwicks (2008). The most impressive cases are those where the patient has been heavily sedated, or in a critical condition, and has roused themselves at the end to recognise deceased family members. This is particularly valuable if it generates information unknown to those in the room which can later be verified.

This is not just a Western phenomenon. Osis and Haraldsson interviewed a substantial sample of doctors and nurses in India as well as in the United States, though in the Indian surveys the visions were often religious figures rather than dead relatives. It is difficult to quantify actual percentages since there may be something of a conspiracy of silence about these things amongst those working in palliative care, or, as a spontaneous case, it may go unnoticed. Yet the Fenwicks stress (2008: 83, 90) that these experiences are not of the same type as hallucinations produced by advanced disease or drugs. They lead to an increase and clarity of consciousness rather than confusion. Yet, the question of hallucination versus veridical apparition and the quality of the evidence will continue to resonate here, as with the Near Death Experience.

The general term 'after death communication' (ADC) has been coined to cover those unbidden and unpredictable experiences of communication with a loved one or friend who has recently died. Often the individuals concerned are reluctant to talk about this, and friends and professionals in the caring industry usually, though not always, interpret the phenomena as subjective and grief-induced. It is quite natural, but also quite wrong, to do so. LaGrand (1997) and Nowotny-Keane (2009), amongst others, have gathered together a number of contemporary accounts. The experiences have sometimes been of voices, smells, presences, but other encounters have been much more palpable and corporeal — actually kissing and touching and seeing the individual concerned. The key evidential issue here, however, is corroboration. Naturally, given the intimacy of the event, the vast majority of the episodes cannot be independently confirmed. However, some of the experiences have been shared by more than one friend or family member and for this reason they are particularly valuable. In addition (as with near death and out of body experiences), the phenomena usually have a profundity and impact on the individual's metaphysical beliefs that go way beyond what one would anticipate from a casual misperception or wished-for self-deception.

It can be breathtaking to discover how easily the sceptical ignore the testimony of remarkable individuals through the ages and the many phenomena associated with them that strongly indicate a non-material, proactive, and creative element to the mind. Probably the most accessible recent compilation of such individuals is the biographical dictionary of Anderson (2006). He is thorough, balanced, and incisive in his approach. He estimates, for example, of the 330 individuals in his book that 50 produced genuinely inexplicable phenomena, a similar number were fraudulent/delusional, and, a wise statement for any researcher, for the remainder there was the lack of clear-cut evidence either way. Leslie Flint (*ibid.*: 60) is a good example of this. The direct voices of the dead appeared to emanate from a region near him, and to many sitters gave persuasive evidence of survival. However, early experiences of what he saw as insensitive testing led him to refuse detailed control later in life. Yet, recordings of a large number of these voices are available on the web through the Leslie Flint educational trust (www.leslieflint.com). It is obviously not possible to test Flint now under controlled conditions to ensure that he did not produce the voices. But it would be perfectly possible to analyse the tapes (and the supporting testimony of sitters) for the quality of their evidence for the survival of the individual concerned. The anecdotal statement that someone had a bad sitting with Flint (Keene, 1976) carries little weight, given the variability of even the best mediums' performances, and can be easily counterbalanced by Aubrey Rose's account of his sittings with the same medium (Rose, 1997: 147–63).

Not everyone has an ADC or an NDE or is lucky enough to have a good sitting with a gifted medium. It has been argued that the developing use of electronic media as a vehicle of communication between the incarnate and discarnate has emerged to allow all, eventually, to access some form of positive experience of this nature which can be recorded and preserved in a permanent, objective form, uncontaminated by the individual idiosyncrasies and fluctuating gifts of the individual medium. The conceptual term covering all this, instrumental transcommunication (ITC), was invented by Ernst Senkowski, a retired German professor of physics. It includes: voices recorded on magnetic tape against a background of white noise from the radio; direct radio voices that erupt spontaneously from the loudspeaker of a radio; images that appear when the television is tuned to an unused channel (sometimes supplemented by video camera projection of the image back on the screen); and communications that come via computers, fax machines, and telephones. A lot of interesting and impressive material has been produced, particularly the dedicated and thoughtful work of Anabela Cardoso. On the other hand, there have been vigorous criticisms of certain aspects of these phenomena. David Ellis has argued that many of the voices can be explained by bleeding in from other radio stations (Ellis, 1978). Others state that the common psychological misperception — pareidolia — the wishful injection of meaning through reading, hearing, seeing of something that just isn't there, is at work. And the most recent survey of one aspect of this field by Boccuzzi and Beischel (2011) has failed to find any clear paranormal element in the phenomena recorded, in that the speech recognition software used was 'unable to detect the phrases perceived by the operator'. This is not, in any way, to denigrate the work of these individuals, it is just that there is not yet the same level, to my mind, of sustained and coherent evidence in this field as exists for more conventional forms of communication, particularly traditional mental and trance mediumship.

Poltergeist outbreaks have been explained in a wide variety of different ways, but in a number of cases a discarnate entity rather than the standard explanation of a mischievous incarnate child of the house, seems, allegedly, responsible. Albert Best was called in on several occasions to try to discover if that was the cause (Cattanach, 2007). In another series of such events, investigated by David Fontana (2005: 80), the incidents seem to have been linked to the death of a young child in the area. There are some remarkable examples of Eileen Garrett's mediumship similarly identifying a 'spirit' as the cause of the disturbances (Angoff, 2009: 91–97). However, these phenomena need to be treated with considerable reservation as it is not difficult to imagine why some people would go to great lengths to fabricate incidents, either because of tensions within the family, or to be re-housed, for example. The standard work by Gauld and Cornell (1979) clearly identifies a number of cases that could fall into that category, but a chapter also examines the question as to whether a discarnate entity (with all the complexity that that phrase masks) was behind the phenomena. They did not, unlike Fontana, come to a positive conclusion (*ibid.*: 359–60).

Raymond Moody (1993) has argued that it is possible for people without mediumistic talents to get in touch with the departed, by employing and expanding on the centuries-old technique of inducing visions from reflective surfaces. He has created what he calls a psychomanteum, in which individuals are invited to immerse themselves first in the character and memories of the person they wish to contact and then physically experience a partially sensory deprived environment in which they will see visions of the departed person in a tilted mirror. Remarkable reports have come from this. However, attempts to replicate this in other centres have had mixed results (Radin, 1997; Parra, 2011), and Moody's original book is short on corroborating detail. A second technique for developing contact with the discarnate has been developed by Botkin (2005) as an initially accidental by-product of his treatment of war veterans with traumatic stress. The technique seems unbelievably simple but has had remarkable effects (*ibid.*: 3–19). However, yet again, the emphasis seems to be on personal, life-changing impact (and certainly none the worse for that!) and Botkin, himself, makes no claims that his work provides scientific evidence for life after death, though others might find it encouraging that hypothesis.

The final category is mind-to-mind and mind-to-environment interaction, and whether or not this can provide evidence supportive of discarnate survival. A fairly intensive reading of some of the historical literature, supplemented by as much of the recent material I was able to access, left me both irritated and dispirited: irritated in the sense that gifted people on all sides of the debate sometimes slipped from their own high standards and demonstrated the weaknesses that they accused others off — lack of insight into the nature of experimental design and control, the use of emotional and polemical language without underpinning evidence, and shifting their ground when either supporting or opposing the psi hypothesis. Particularly instructive recent examples of this are the articles in Krippner and Friedman's book (2010) on the existence of psychic phenomena. But a couple of positive points seem to me to emerge from this rancorous debate: firstly, that in the Ganzfeld protocol and research one has a tool which appears to be consistently generating a paranormal effect — limited, true, but definitely above chance (Carter, in Krippner and Friedman, 2010: 159–60) — and this has been confirmed by a later review (Williams, B.J., 2011). This is the crucial point and not the *argumentum ad hominem* on both sides and dubious speculation about the psychological flaws that prevent sceptics from accepting good evidence and allow those supporting the existence of psi to engage in quasi-magical thinking. The other major field where there seems to be substantial and replicable (in a broad sense) evidence for the action of the mind other than through the normal senses is remote viewing (Utts, 1995): but certainly not from all those who profess to practise it and train others in it. Russell Targ recounts, in vivid detail, his several decades research into this and the evidence for his positive conclusions (Targ, 2012).

Two massive and impressive books, *Irreducible Mind* (Kelly *et al.*, 2007) and *The Synchronised Universe/Life Force* (Swanson, 2009, 2011, 2 vols.), have, in recent years, surveyed in much greater scholarly and scientific detail the topics mentioned above. The former (building on earlier work and support by Michael Murphy, 1992, of the Esalen Institute) challenges 'the view from the mainstream' that a reductive biological materialism will fully explain consciousness. The book, in exhaustive detail, points out that the many examples of mind influencing body reported in Myers' day have been confirmed by later research—stigmata, the physical influence of multiple personality on handwriting and eyesight, painless surgery under hypnosis, healing of skin conditions including warts, etc. It also criticises (as did Tallis as we have seen) neuroscientific fundamentalism, and after a review of near death experiences and related phenomena, genius, and mystical states, proposes a theory for mind–body relations based on the work of Myers and James and a particular interpretation of quantum theory which it classifies as a kind of non-Cartesian interactive dualism. The authors believe that the fundamentally sound outline model of the mind posited by Myers and James, which was sidelined by the twin attack from Freudianism and Behaviourism in the twentieth century, will increasingly be confirmed by research, and that we should have the courage, based on empirical rigour, to embrace 'the supernormal and transpersonal phenomena that are essential to a fuller understanding of human mind and personality' (Kelly *et al.*, 2007: 643).

As a physicist, Swanson has tried to pull together the growing empirical scientific evidence for the underpinning force of the universe, the original creative substance that is both mind and matter, and which, he argues, lies behind the phenomena discussed in this book. His work, however, crucially raises the question of replication and comparing like with like. For example, he takes a view of Kirlian photography which is totally at odds with the experiments of

Arthur Ellison, a professor of electrical engineering (2002: 224-26). On the other hand, B.O. Williams (2010) has argued that more recent computerised approaches to Kirlian imaging have got round these problems and produced more consistent, measurable results.

Many in the mainstream may call Swanson's work pseudo-scientific, even 'pathological science', but the need to examine the evidence in detail still remains. Moreover, Swanson is not what one would call a New Age flake. He was educated at MIT and Princeton Universities and for many years worked in scientific consulting carrying out studies in applied physics for commercial and government agencies (Swanson, 2011, vol. 2: 629). His theories are based on direct field research, laboratory experimentation, and a wide-ranging literature search from both Western and Eastern sources. He puts forward a synchronized universe model which he realistically calls 'a collection of interesting and promising ideas which have not yet been proven'. He argues that at the quantum level electrons and other particles become synchronized to a particular phase and frequency which, under the right conditions, provides the energy and structure of OBEs, NDEs, remote viewing, apparitions, mediumship, and healing, etc. However, his fundamental point is that these forces are most effectively released and deployed in a spirit of love and constructive thinking: at root the universe is spiritual.

6. Given positive results from the above lines of enquiry, does this necessarily mean that the source of the information is a discarnate personality?

A good reading can be very persuasive and the sitter can leave glowing from the sense of communion with a discarnate friend or relative. However, in the light of our lack of detailed knowledge about the nature of the paranormal and the conditions under which it occurs, other possible hypotheses need to be reviewed, particularly the super-psi theory discussed below. I shall first, however, consider the arguments in favour of the survival hypothesis. (Hart, 1959, has a good overview of the issue.) Researchers who have studied mediums in great depth tend to favour the survival hypothesis because of the almost overwhelming sense of individual personality that comes from a high quality trance mediumship reading and sometimes from mental mediumship. I give one example, that of James Hyslop.

Hyslop was an absolutely indefatigable American researcher and he considered the super-psi versus survival issue in some detail, in his rather dense and knotty prose, in an enormous part of the *Proceedings of the SPR* (Hyslop, 1901) devoted to his work with Mrs Piper. In it Hyslop (*ibid.*: 289–97) argued that explaining away survival on the basis of a combination of telepathy/clairvoyance/multiple personality did not stand up on several grounds. I summarise his main points:

- The resemblances between multiple personality and what was actually going on in a Piper trance were superficial
- Telepathy, as known experimentally, had never shown the ability to produce the convincing dramatic productions of trance mediumship
- The impressive unity of consciousness displayed by the best communicators in terms of specific facts and their memories and the distinct discrimination between different sitters 'in spite of the way they are sandwiched in for sittings, and the synthetic complexity of the facts given'
- 'The dramatic interplay of different personalities, the personal traits of the communicator, the emotional tone that was natural to the same, the proper appreciation of a situation or a question'
- And he laid down the challenge that, if people put forward super-psi as the explanation, 'I shall exact of them the production of the same specific and experimental evidence for the truth and explanatory power of their assumptions that we have presented in the

Piper phenomena', and to show that 'telepathy, with its adjuncts, can reproduce as perfectly the personal identity of a living consciousness as Mrs Piper produces that of the deceased'.

Kennedy (1974: 96–97) makes an interesting point in the debate between telepathy and survival as an explanation for communication. He mentions that he had no communication, via Albert Best (who kept saying he was getting nothing), from his wife for at least two months after her death. Had the impetus been telepathy from the living (that is his yearning need for contact), communication would have started immediately since all the memories were available in his mind. He argues that much literature on the subject points to this period of delay as the personality adjusts to a new environment. This seems quite plausible, though those who have died suddenly or violently or young often seem able to communicate immediately.

Some psychical researchers have tried to crack this impasse by exhaustively examining cases to see if any of them cannot fully be explained by the super-psi hypothesis. Berger (2010) has worked painstakingly through this issue by examining thirty cases, some old classic ones and some relatively recent ones. He rightly points out that we can only have evidence beyond more or less reasonable doubt and that when we have considered all the other explanations it tends to be the sense of individual character and purpose that convinces us. Schwartz in his book (2011: 347–48) also discusses the alternatives and, while he admits that much of the information is consistent with super-psi, asserts that information not known to the sitter is often given and that, even though one might posit a cosmic data base as the source, the retrieval of that information is so organised and expressed that it is strongly suggestive of the personality and continuing intentions of the deceased.

In fact it has been strongly argued (Roy, 2008) that the most impressive example of such sophisticated organisation is what, as mentioned earlier, has come to be called the cross-correspondences. It is asserted that after their deaths the early leaders of the SPR constructed a set of experiments (contained in 2,500 scripts produced by automatic writing) to get round the super-psi hypothesis, though they would not have called it that. These scripts consisted of messages or parts of messages transmitted to two or more mediums that only made complete sense when put together and studied carefully. The material is highly complex and there is always the possibility of reading too much into it. However, there are many persuasive examples of apparent design, selection, and organisation contained in the scripts, and Saltmarsh (1976) has produced a very useful and clear summary of a number of these. One of the mediums involved, Mrs Coombe-Tennant, apparently communicated after her death through another highly gifted automatist, Geraldine Cummins (1965), and the resultant book, *Swan on a Black Sea*, is, in terms of conveying the full dramatic impact of a personality, one of the most impressive examples of its type. However (see Barrington, 1966), there is always the question of how much Cummins knew normally about Coombe-Tennant.

The after death communications of Elizabeth Targ provide a related, though not exact, parallel. In this case, the discarnate communicator appeared spontaneously to a variety of contacts around the world: to her father's partner, Jane Katra; to a nursing professor at Duke University; to a woman in Norway; a sick woman in Switzerland; and in other locations. One of the main purposes seemed to be to provide the spiritual healing support that, after an initially powerful scepticism, she had come to believe in shortly before her death (Katra, 2011), but, as with the cross-correspondences, it also suggests a purposive discarnate intelligence with a particular agenda and not 'mere' telepathy or clairvoyance.

There is an argument (Vandersande, 2008: 8) that the evidence from physical mediumship is very persuasive evidence for survival as opposed to psi. However, the fraudulent possibilities are obvious, and even the most impressive examples have their critics. Louie Harris's book (2009), on her husband Alec Harris, shines with sincerity, as does Remmers' (1967) and Tom Harrison's (2004), but the phenomena are beyond my boggle threshold, and that of most people I would imagine. Cornell (2002), indeed, has written a rather dismissive account of one of Alec Harris's sittings at Cardiff which is in stark contrast with the experiences of other people. As a very seasoned investigator, Cornell's views must be taken seriously (*ibid.*: 327–38). He stated that the materialised spirit that approached him was all too material—it had a rumbling stomach (which he noticed Harris had when he came into the room) and nicotine-smelling breath. It is frankly impossible to reconcile this account with those in Louie Harris's book. I freely admit that my prejudices are showing, but there are very few accounts of physical mediumship one can take seriously until it has been clearly demonstrated in the light, or if that is not allowed, using thermal imaging techniques.

However, very recently the Victor Zammit website has consistently recorded positive accounts of sittings with David Thompson and the Circle of the Silver Cord (backed by a number of detailed and supportive reports by general sitters, academics, and psychical researchers), and the Felix Experimental Group in Germany has produced, in partial light, some interesting phenomena. Yet, two final points. Inevitably, the Thompson sittings have attracted some criticism—the most searching (if his account of the event is accurate) by Roy Stemman, a highly experienced writer on Spiritualism (see Zammit, Felix Experimental Group, and Stemman websites on this debate). And secondly, physical phenomena alone are not in themselves proof of the survival of individual consciousness. Myers and Barrett (1889) in their detailed review of the literature on Daniel Dunglas Home, possibly the greatest British physical medium of them all, lamented the failure of many of the sitters to demand or follow up on specific evidence of identity from the 'spirits' (Myers and Barrett, 1889: 116-17).

Another attempt to break the super-psi vs. survival blockade has been through what are called compact cases: that is, while alive an individual promises to communicate after his or her death. Evidence of this return can be either through some form of sensory identification (a vision, a voice, etc.), or more complexly, by conveying, through a medium, the contents of a message put in a sealed envelope when alive, by giving the key to a code set up when alive, or by some other similar test. Provided the information is not accessed by a clairvoyant while the individual is still alive, the likelihood of a discarnate source is allegedly increased. Celebrated psychical researchers, past and present, have tried this but the evidential record of such activity is mixed. Myers examined (1904, vol. 2: 43-51) twelve occasions when such a compact was fulfilled but, in his own case, the result was rather confusing—no direct hit but material of powerful, allusive relevance to the actual message (Salter, 1958). Oliver Lodge also provided sealed documents whose contents he intended to communicate post-mortem. Only one medium, Geraldine Cummins, came close to an approximation of the contents.[10] Neither have recent efforts been any more successful. The educational psychologist and psychical researcher, R.H. Thouless, set up a couple of cipher tests to which he would provide the key after his death. In one sitting with a medium he stated that he had forgotten it and, in 1995, one of the codes was broken by computer, thus rather defeating the purpose (Oram, 1998: 158-59). Susy Smith (2000b: 228-30) established a project—the Afterlife Codes—to do something similar on a larger scale, using the World Wide Web. But the project seems to have petered out.

---

[10] Lodge devised (with the best of intentions) a hideously over-complicated protocol to guide mediums towards the content of his documents. Cummins was given some help in her efforts to reveal Lodge's message (Firebrace and Gay, 1955).

The Revd Dr Charles Fryer (Perry and Fontana, 2009) also tried to communicate a message that had not been cracked by sensitives during his lifetime—it was a seven line poem—this too was unsuccessful. Ian Stevenson also left a cipher to which he intended to communicate a key after death. This was in 2007 and to date no result. Probably the most famous successful example in the literature is a case quoted by Myers (1904, vol. 2: 182–85) in which a woman's cousin, Benja, communicated (as he said he would before death) where he had hidden a piece of brick with a message contained in it and what the message said. The communication came from a table tipping session at home with just the woman and her mother present—the table tipped or tilted at the relevant letter of the alphabet when it was called out. Examples like this inspired Myers (1892) in his most grandiloquent language to put the question:

> Why should not every death-bed be made the starting point of a long experiment? And why should not every friend who sails forth…—into the unknown sea—endeavour to send us news from that bourne from which few travellers, perhaps, have as yet made any adequate or systematic preparation to return?

For any such activity does face considerable problems and one wonders if it is worth the effort. Firstly, as Myers pointed out, any promise to return to a particular individual may be doomed 'on account of the surviving friend's lack of appropriate sensitivity'. And, it further follows, the medium's. Secondly, we have no knowledge, except through mediumistic communications, of the conditions of putative discarnate existence, and what information we do have suggests that the transmission of precise and complicated information is exceedingly difficult. 'Myers', through Geraldine Cummins (1967: 106), stated that we lose the detail of our cognitive memories after death (though not our emotional memories and affinities), and that it is an effort to 'resuscitate' and then communicate them to the incarnate. Thirdly, no matter how ingenious the code and stunning the communication of the solution, the result will always be susceptible to explanation by retrocognitive or precognitive clairvoyance or telepathy (Oram, 1998: 158). We have to recognise that there is no way round the problem, except the accumulation of evidence that consistently and in unambiguous detail demonstrates planning, purpose, and compassion in the discarnate communicator. Berger (1987) has discussed these points in some detail, with a slightly different focus, concentrating on those qualities that might make for a good, discarnate communicator.

Turning to the arguments against the survival hypothesis: a remarkable thing one discovers is that communicators at sittings are not always what they seem (Roll, 1974). At one session the psychical researcher Dr Soal had with the medium Blanche Cooper, Gordon Davis, an old school friend, came through and provided evidence of his identity by way of memories of his old school. All well and good, but Soal later discovered Davis was very much alive and was having business meetings at the time of the sitting. This would suggest some form of telepathic transmission from the subconscious of a living agent which provides, in conjunction with the energies of the sitter and the medium, an associative cluster, which may have some temporary independent mental life.

The Gordon Davis case highlights the fact that we know very little about the boundaries and limits of psi, as Braude rightly points out (1992), and the range and power of the subconscious mind. So the counter-hypothesis to survival, stated in its fullest form, postulates that a combination of clairvoyance, telepathy, retro- and precognitive abilities, plus the ability to affect the material world—psychokinesis—all combined with dramatic gifts of impersonation, based on the medium's own plasticity and dissociation of consciousness (even extending to the level of multiple personality disorder), can adequately account for the phenomena that appear to point to the survival of the individual personality after death. Therefore, no matter how specific the information, how persuasive the sense of individual purpose, presence, and personality, no matter how rich and complex the gifts displayed, particularly in trance mediumship, there is always this alternative, and we have no way of deciding between the two.

Ducasse (1962), however, does not believe that living psi can explain those cases where discarnates demonstrate specific mental skills (knowledge in the sense of knowledge how to) characteristic of them in life. Braude (1992) argues that he has no right to make that distinction. We just do not know. In addition, Sudduth (2009) has asserted that the survivalist interpretation relies on the operation of a kind of psi 'that is indistinguishable from what is required by the super-psi hypothesis'. We have no idea how living mediums or discarnate entities navigate through and select from this vast body of information, and have no warrant, as Gauld (1982) does, in assuming that the complexity of the task leads one to favour the survival over the super-psi hypothesis. Moreover, the argument that the survival hypothesis is scientific because it is falsifiable and the super-psi hypothesis is unscientific because it is unfalsifiable is untenable (Fontana, 2005: 110–11). At one level of generality both are unfalsifiable and unscientific, and at more specific levels aspects of both theories can be framed in terms of testable hypotheses.

In fact, the most sensible conclusion (given that one accepts that psi exists at all) is to hypothesise that at different times and under different conditions and according to the needs and purposes of the living and the discarnate, energy we call psi can be utilised and manipulated. Matthew Manning's career is an excellent example of this. Manning (1974), as a young man, experienced an enormous variety of psi phenomena: psychokinesis, automatic writing and drawing, poltergeists, apparent communication from discarnate personalities, etc. He eventually came to the conclusion that the most effective solution for his peace of mind and personal development was to channel the energy that he strongly suspected was generating the phenomena into healing (Manning, 1999). This he did with very positive results both for himself and others.

Powell (2010) has argued that the impasse will remain until data are collected that can distinguish between the two explanations. The traditional approach has been to continue to collect and analyse those cases that are both extremely convincing in terms of high quality evidence of individual identity and of design, purpose, control, and selection in the provision and framing of that evidence. A more innovative attempt to break the deadlock is that of Beischel/Rock (2009). They have launched a phenomenological research project to try to ascertain whether or not mediums' experience of discarnate contact is different from their experience of telepathy and clairvoyance with the living. If this is consistently the case, and if it is regularly associated with the provision of good quality survival evidence, the balance could tip towards the survival hypothesis. This, interestingly, may well confirm the unpublished research of Fontana, Keen and Roy (Fontana, 2005: 107) that most mediums notice distinct differences in the exercise of psychic or mediumistic abilities.[11] A third strategy, building on Vandersande's point above, is to support the development of high quality physical mediumship under safe and secure conditions and with due regard for the medium's well-being. Finally, a recent and intriguing approach is Rousseau's (2012), arguing that certain features of the near death experience, particularly those involving very young children, may further load the scales in favour of the survival hypothesis.

7. Is it possible to identify those conditions which make for successful sittings, and what are the implications of this for

---

[11] An unpublished study for the Prism-Psychical Research Involving Selected Mediums Group.

the guidance and training of sitters, mediums, and researchers?

I mentioned in Part 1 my rather dispiriting experience of a training workshop in mediumship and spirit awareness. But I increasingly came to realise how unfair some of my criticisms were. Firstly, any trainer working in the broad areas of psychology, social science, counselling, etc. is involved with soft, qualitative, fuzzy issues and can only offer a range of approaches that may not be effective for the individuals concerned. Secondly, a related point, we have models in our minds of the way science and technology operate — practical and applied solutions based on sound observation and theory — and if we invest in something we expect to see it in operation and to be able to measure the impact. William Barrett, one of the founders of the SPR, stressed (regarding telepathy and other 'powers' investigated) that the crucial issue was the identification of the conditions under which these strange things occurred. But it is one thing to observe that they do occur, another to establish under which conditions, and a third to find any kind of explanation for them all!

Yet how can we train people if we don't know how something works and how to explain it? For example, one standard model of scientific explanation is Hempel's covering law theory (Papineau, in Grayling, 2004: 171–73). We establish a set of conditions that lead to a particular event, and this event is explained by a particular law that covers the situation. Many small such instances can go to build up the comprehension of large-scale phenomena. The thing to be explained can be deduced from the original inductive observations plus the law, and given the same conditions we can predict the future occurrence of the event. Moreover, even if the event does not materialise (snow, a failed experiment) we can usually work out why by revisiting the observation of the conditions and the application of the law. There will, of course, be many situations in which physical laws intersect with large populations of people (as in medicine and disease) and, therefore, a probabilistic interpretation of the covering law theory will operate since it is not possible to identify all the conditions and the interrelationships.

When we try to apply such a model to the training of mediums we immediately run into problems. Such a model works when the training is for the repair of car engines or, generally, human bodies. But what, if any, knowledge, skill, and understanding can be imparted at training sessions for mediums to, to put it crudely, summon up the spirits of the dead? What language can we use? What forces, concepts, laws, can we invoke? Are we trapped forever in the endless deployment of *energies* and *vibrations*? Tart (2009: 109) and Symthies (2000: 242-44) have pointed out the difficulties in trying to treat psi forces as a form of electromagnetism. Stated like this the situation is absurd but unfortunately the above model, in a hazy and unformulated form, is the kind of mental premise that most people operate on, and it is not discouraged by the extravagant claims in some of the Spiritualist literature on training and development, even though disclaimers are nowadays in place because psychic and mediumistic activities have recently come under the consumer protection law. In fact, given the above issues, training is probably the wrong term: coaching, facilitation, guidance, critical friend (in the best sense of critical) are probably more appropriate words.

Irritation with the lack of a theoretical underpinning to help understand, explain, and possibly predict the kind of conditions favourable to the paranormal, can understandably tempt people into premature and sometimes grandiose speculation. This can be intellectually stimulating but may put off the very communities it is designed to appeal to: for example, Clarke and King (2006) have criticised the misapplication of concepts like the zero point field to the psi area, and Jahn/Dunne (2011) have likewise objected to the misapplication of quantum theory concepts by some, though by no means all, researchers in the field of the paranormal. In addition, Walker (2000: 107) has pointed out the absurdity of using Everett's Many-Worlds version of quantum theory to suggest that there might be contact between these worlds — and by implication that paranormal phenomena might be explained in this way.

In empirical terms, the amount of recent research into the process of mediumship and the implications for training is miniscule. There is no current sustained enquiry over twenty or thirty years into mediums as there was with Mrs Piper, Mrs Leonard, and Mrs Garrett. Hatton (2010), to some extent blames the mediums, since so few of them seem prepared to cooperate with scientists in joint investigations. This split goes right back to the founding of the SPR when, in their absolutely correct desire to weed out fraud and wishful thinking, the early researchers alienated part of the Spiritualist movement. This tension, reflecting different ways of knowing and defining truth (the anecdotal and first-hand versus the academic, critical, and distanced) must be resolved (Hamilton 2009: 112). It is true that in the UK the Spiritualists' National Union mount a range of training programmes, but these, no doubt admirable in practical terms, do not seem to make much use of the insights of psychologists and parapsychologists.

In this most sensitive of areas one would hope that people of good will, and above all genuine talent, might come together and work on a number of research themes that would yield real benefit. But there are caveats. Firstly, high quality mediumship appears to be a rare gift. Secondly, it is no respecter of education and social class, as Hatton again points out. This means that researchers (and there are some unfortunate counter-examples) need to show great tact, courtesy, and sensitivity, and above all to establish a genuine rapport while retaining the necessary distance and objectivity.

How far researchers go down the road to actual participant observation is a matter for them in each context. Mackian (2011: 27–29) has graphically recounted the tensions that can develop (despite university protocols stipulating mutual respect) when active involvement in marginal and anomalous research is recounted,

> But angels don't exist do they, so how can they heal? That's just ridiculous!

However, there have been signs in recent years in the UK that such a rapprochement is gradually developing. Gilbert has researched the experiential properties of contemporary spirit mediumship and Roxburgh has studied the psychology and phenomenology of mediumship (Gilbert, 2007: 29). Roxburgh has also taken part in mediumship training at the Arthur Findlay College, the training centre of the Spiritualists' National Union (Roxburgh, 2006: 18–23). But there is still more to investigate in depth. As Alvarado (2009) has put it, 'much needs to be done regarding the study of mediumistic imagery, and of the dynamics of subconscious aspects of mediumship'. It could be argued that mediums ought to experience, at the very least, some training programme that has the humanity and spirituality of, for example, Assagioli's *Psychosynthesis* (1993) and its post-Freudian dynamic enrichment of the concept of the subconscious mind (*ibid*.: 16–20).

The fundamental issue is that there has been a lack of generous and imaginative appreciation of both the nature of mediumship and the difficult stresses and strains that there are on those who practise it. Firstly, the medium may be scarred by the hostile pressures from earlier in his/her life. Secondly, they may have sensitivity, whether supernormal or not, which makes certain people, places, and conditions problematic as variables in their work. Thirdly, the gift is bound to be variable and fluctuating. Fourthly, they have no control over the sitters—hostile, disturbed, conflicted—and unless they are sitting under the protective roof of an established organisation (e.g. SAGB, CPS), or demonstrating before an audience, there is always the (thankfully remote) possibility of physical or mental abuse. Fifthly, they (at least in the UK) operate under an ambiguous and patronising legal framework. In the media they are treated as psychic entertainers. When giving sittings, they come under the consumer law and issues of possible false claims and fraud are paramount. Such environments are hardly conducive to the best communications. It makes one long for the protective environment in which Mrs Piper and Mrs Leonard were able to work—with an income guaranteed and supportive researchers and administrators about them.

One would hope that there would be a merging of as many intellectual perspectives and practices in this field as possible. A considerable body of research on learning and communication styles and multiple intelligences, which has built up in recent years, can be utilised (Gardner, 1985). Researchers and trainers could particularly learn from the world of experiential and vocational education and training, where well developed techniques for recognising tacit and implicit practical and intuitive knowledge and making it explicit for the improvement of self and others' performance has long been recognised (Kolb, 1984). There is the huge growth in the field of sports coaching and human development (Murphy, 1992), particularly working with top performing individuals and learning lessons from them. It is also important to cooperate with mediums who show reflective insight into their own processes, and for someone to do for mental mediumship what Pamela Rae Heath (2010: 163–258) has done for physical phenomena.

However, the relationship between mediums and professionals who work in the psychological, health care, social work, and training and development fields can be highly problematic and requires a sensitive, open, and mutually respectful approach. There are issues of licensing/certification and training to deal with, as well as the particularly thorny matter of the alignment of mediumship practice to the standards of care that operate in many professions. Goforth (2011) has identified the huge variability of approaches and the way in which some practitioners (by no means inevitably fraudulent) use other qualifications as a proxy to demonstrate their respectability. He has done groundbreaking work in highlighting many of the key issues.

The Windbridge Institute in the United States, led by Julie Beischel, is one of the very few scientific organisations trying to deal with these matters in a practical and rigorous way (the Division of Perceptual Studies at the University of Virginia, particularly the work of Emily Williams Kelly, is another). There is much to commend in their approach, with its code of ethics and training in grief counselling built into it. However, terminology is important in the messages it sends out, and to talk about a level 5 certified Windbridge medium smacks, almost laughably, of the excesses of certain cults and suggests an unrealistic precision in an inevitably imprecise field. The institute has also been criticised for not separating out the training and the research function (mediums eager to gain certification might tend to give the answers that the researchers want), and for not creating a sufficiently rich and supportive phenomenological environment (Roxborough *et al.*, 2009). Some of this criticism seems unfair, however, given the geographical and ideological environment in which they have to operate. Nevertheless, enriching their data collection methods from other sources, like extensive published accounts by mediums of their own experiences and processes (Emmons, 2003; Rubinstein, 2011) would be of value.[12]

In terms of the content of such programmes, the core training focus should probably continue to be on both the development and interpretation of appropriate imagery and sensory information, and the fostering of attitudes that still the mind and make it receptive to such inputs. This should be based, as stated above, on the work and experience of the best practitioners, and it should adopt a phenomenological

---

[12] No one has treated these issues with greater sensitivity and insight, based on many years of sitting with mediums, than Paul Beard (1992). His work is still worth reading as a guide to process and a support for training.

approach which allows participants to recognise and foster the states conducive to psi (both general and specific to the individual). However, recent work by Rock *et al.* (2011) has suggested that the development of techniques for cultivating visual imagery may be more important for psi than just stilling the chatter of the mind; and a more eclectic and wide-ranging approach to both philosophy and training methods may well produce dividends. See the work of Roney-Dougal, for example (2010).

Three final points. Sometimes one thinks that some of the researchers who engage in this field have a breathtakingly simple model of the nature of communication. All the evidence suggests that it is difficult, that conditions can vary considerably. The power of the signal seems to vary greatly and even when strong it is difficult to interpret single and mixed sensory experiences accurately, to distinguish literal from symbolic images, and to discern which aspects of the information provided have most relevance and meaning for the sitter. These points are brought out in Hart (1959: 86–88). In addition, it is not easy to be a good sitter and, at the least, guidance if not training should be provided here. Also, researchers should strictly follow the ethical guidelines on research with human and animal participants that their institutions have in place and, hopefully, have had appropriate sensitivity training themselves.

It is worth amplifying the point on sitter guidance. In all my/our sittings there was very little attention paid to informing the sitter as to the nature of the experience and how they could contribute to the process (except for a short leaflet from the College of Psychic Studies). Too often the sitter is passive, bemused, and unable to respond when the medium says,

Have you any questions you'd like to ask them?

Finally, sports people and actors and musicians often go over their performances again and again in order to improve them. Though one intuitively feels that the necessary condition is the will and capacity of a discarnate entity to communicate, much could surely be done by a detailed analysis of transcripts and video tapes. That is one reason I have published pretty full accounts of each of my/our sittings. For my part it was an attempt to analyse the evidence in detail rather than just leave the reader with an impressionistic feel. But the revisiting of a full audio/video performance also has the merit of revealing to a reflective medium where his or her performance may have faltered because of a tired, unthinking phrase or two, or failure to follow up on a key intuition.

8. What does evidence from mediumship tell us about the nature and experience of the 'we' that might survive, and are there any lessons we can draw from this as to how we should live our lives here and now?

Gauld helpfully discusses the first part of this question in a review of Patterson's book on the subject (Gauld, 1998).

For many, possibly most, people, personal identity is intimately, perhaps inextricably, linked to the body one inhabits, and Gauld argues that, of the marks of personal identity used in legal and historical cases, that of spatio-temporal track (the actual body in time) trumps all others. Without such a track, after death, can all the other evidence realistically be given a survivalist interpretation, and can the endless accumulation of evidence get round this problem? However, for a significant percentage of the world population, the question of personal identity and personal body is not a problem. This position is held by certain Christian traditions which believe, like the great 18th century chemist Joseph Priestley (Knight, 2004), that the true Christian doctrine is 'not the immortality of the soul but of the resurrection of the body' (*ibid.*: 10) in all its full sensory awareness and fleshly vitality. Emily Dickinson has beautifully written of such dead waiting for the full and eternal restoration of their bodies:

Safe in their alabaster chambers
Sleep the meek members of the resurrection.

On the other hand, H.H. Price (1953) has argued that survival might well be like the world of dreams but more substantial and coherent—a world of thought images that reflects the tastes, affinities, beliefs, ethics, hopes, and fears that we have developed in our incarnate life. He puts forward this thesis to provide a coherent concept of an unembodied identity and to counter the argument that to talk about a person without their body is logically inconsistent. Building on earlier ideas, he postulates an ether of images in which individual consciousnesses that have certain associative affinities would survive. And he argues that such an environment would appear real since the images would be auditory, tactile, and kinaesthetic as well. This accords quite well with much in Spiritualistic literature. It also has the advantage of linking to those phenomena, as we have seen in earlier sections, that have shown living individuals receiving information through images which they could not normally have received through the five senses. One problem, of course, is that the comparison to dream states can only be partial since the dreamer's sleep is in an embodied form, and physicalists would argue that there is no evidence for such imagistic experience without a neurophysiological base to generate them.

Another issue is that Price does not really consider the organising structure for the collection of images making up the disembodied person. Broad has argued that these disembodied images might be temporary and lack coherence and stability (1925: 536–38). He speculates that an unconscious psychic factor may detach itself at death and when it comes in contact with a medium or sensitive the experiences of the deceased will be re-activated, giving the semblance but not the reality of individual consciousness. An awful thought: withered psychic leaves temporarily animated by the vitality of a living medium. There is, however, a long tradition in occult literature, and analysed in the work of Robert Crookall (1960, 1961), that suggests a structure that pulls these things together. Inside each human being nests, like Russian dolls, several bodies—physical, etheric, astral, mental, spiritual (Crookall uses different terms)—and each of these bodies has to be adjusted to, and is appropriate for, a particular stage of development. This theory would reconcile different perspectives and experiences and explain confused and disorganised communication: and that the spirit consciousness has to train itself to gain control over that unstable and mysterious world. However, Swanson (2011) states that attempts to prove the existence of such a structure by measurement rather than by the intuitive perceptions of sensitives is problematic.

A more robust account of such a position is Lawton's article (2010) on the Scientific and Medical Network website. He argues that these subtle bodies are real (*ibid.*: 3), that 'There is bodily survival of bodily death', and that the postmortem body can, under certain circumstances, physically impact on the material world but normally resides in a higher dimensional space–time. He quotes a substantial body of material, of varying degrees of plausibility, to support this. Augustine (2011), however, has severely criticised the concept of the astral body when considering possible vehicles for the survival of the personality; largely it has to be said on the grounds of its inherent absurdity, the idea of astral clothes, the astral plane, and the concept of the astral body as an exact duplicate of the physical body. Nevertheless, he does concede that a modified theory of the astral body that is not an exact mirror of the physical body is not conceptually impossible.[13]

In fact, in recent years one has seen a revival of interest in the concept of subtle bodies (Gustus, 2011). Gustus's book summarises the life-long research (based on intensive personal experience) of the Brazilian doctor Waldo Vieira into

---

[13] Historical and anecdotal accounts of seeing another person's astral body can be surprisingly concrete. Joan Miller saw the astral body of her MI5 boss, Maxwell Knight, on one occasion (Miller, 1986). Quite a useful tool in MI5's armoury one would have thought! See also Alvarado (2011).

out of body experiences and the nature of consciousness generally. It is argued that anyone, with sufficient training and persistence, can detach the extraphysical (astral) body from the physical, and that this provides transformative personal proof of survival. In addition, Vieira (as summarised by Gustus) has developed a broad and encompassing metaphysics which explains automatic writing, mediumship, clairvoyance, etc. and supports the spiritual development of the individual. However, while fascinating reading, the book does not provide the documentary base — that is, research evidence that clearly demonstrates that veridical perceptions are taking place out of body — and until that happens one has to be very cautious as to the ontological status of the material.

So, regardless of one's form out of body or in the afterlife, what evidence do we have as to its nature? One can, of course, read any number of accounts that purport to describe what the discarnate state is like, based on mediums' reports, and channelled and automatic writing. There has been a flurry of interesting and useful material on this in recent years (Heath and Klimo, 2010; Fontana, 2009; Tymn, 2011a). And I have found at least one website that has attempted to gather and coordinate descriptions of the afterlife — AECES (see page 113). It does strike one that there is broad agreement in these accounts in terms of the nature of consciousness that leaves at death and its post-mortem experiences. There is the sense of a process of gradual refinement as the spirit develops further into the higher levels of consciousness. However, while there is a level of consistency in these accounts there are many non-paranormal explanations for that consistency, and there needs to be a greater rigour in checking both the quality of the information provided and the credentials of the 'communicator', and the matching of them against each other.

Two examples: William James is supposed to have communicated both through Susy Smith (2000a) and Jane Roberts (1978). Why through both mediums, and is there any evidence that this was a designed strategy? Do the two 'William James's' credibly seem to be the same personality, given the fact that each medium obviously colours and flavours the transmission in the light of their individual character and abilities? Has any factual historical material been transmitted that 'proves' the credentials of the source? In particular, does any of the automatic writing shed light on the working life, practice, and academic preoccupations of the incarnate James? The incarnate James would certainly have insisted on some such. Secondly, there is the case of R.H. Benson allegedly communicating through Anthony Borgia (1954). The books produced in this fashion have been widely read and well received in the Spiritualist community. Benson was the catholic convert son of the late 19th-century Archbishop of Canterbury, E.W. Benson. R.H. Benson attacked Spiritualism in his life, and the alleged discarnate Benson expresses contriteness, in some of his communications, at these anti-Spiritualistic outbursts. That part is true. But Benson had, when alive, some unpleasant characteristics, and one would have thought that there would have been, in his spiritual progress and growth, some recognition of that in the communications (Askwith, 1973: 213-17). I have not found this or any other evidential material. But I freely admit that I have, however, not read the full body of automatic writings transmitted by Borgia and may have missed certain things.

Finally, we may have to accept that the nature of the post-mortem self is far more complex than we usually believe. We have learned through Myers, James, Janet, Freud, and Jung that, in this life, we are not always the logical and self-controlled individual we think we are, and that we contain a variety of competing sub-personalities differing in their drives, perceptions, values, durations, and intensities. But many of us find even that difficult to credit because the physical demands and frameworks of life provide an illusory solidity and grounding. What if the situation after death is even more liquid and variable? I have found myself attracted to the writings of Professor Michael Whiteman (1986; Poynton, 2011) who, based on his own personal experience and detailed and subtle analysis of it, has suggested that the idea of a single core self, isolated from and unaffected by other spiritual beings, both in this life and beyond, is too naïve. This would fit in with Myers' views, articulated in a number of different contexts, that each individual personality is part of a much larger group soul. The group soul may be small, almost a family group, and/or considerably larger, based on common interests, tasks, and affinities. For the purpose of communicating with and encouraging our incarnate friends and relatives we present an identifiable 'persona', but we are not trapped in it, we evolve and grow as part of the greater group, and only particular facets of that group incarnate, when necessary, to learn specific spiritual lessons through appropriate physical experiences. There is quite surprising consistency in the best afterlife reports about this. But it is an unprovable internal consistency, persuasive only by the quality of the insight and the communication, neither verifiable nor falsifiable.

One area of Whiteman's thought is particularly contentious and possibly alarming—that is his thesis based on the reading of Swedenborg and his own detailed introspection that while incarnate we may be influenced strongly by discarnate spirits, and feelings, experiences, dreams, moods that we claim as our own may actually be a composite of ours and theirs. This is a step too far for me, and my emotional reaction is that it smacks too much of pre-enlightenment thinking, but it is a concept that has been taken seriously by a number of reflective and balanced individuals. Ultimately this raises the question of barriers and filters between individual personalities both incarnate and discarnate. What James (1986: 374) has called 'the conditions of individuation or insulation'. Is the universe structured according to a set of increasingly permeable parameters—the earthly, the early discarnate, the evolved discarnate, and the ultimate discarnate state? The ultimate discarnate state being one in which all barriers are dissolved between advanced spiritual consciousnesses that have purged themselves of the dross of lower levels.

What are the implications of all this for how we should live our lives here and now? I can only really answer for myself. The moral lesson is clear and comes through all the high quality material in this field: the importance of living one's life in the light of kindness, tolerance, and love, and which is not necessarily expressed in grand gestures but through small, daily, unprompted acts of affection and sympathy. The intellectual lesson is one of discrimination: the need to distinguish between adequate and inadequate evidence, the shunning of the fraudulent and the self-deluded, and the importance of never surrendering one's own capacity for judgment and decision making to anyone else, whether guru or alleged spirit. There may well be a case for some form of post-mortem survival, but that should not lead to a return to pre-enlightenment values. As Myers, himself, suggested on more than one occasion, love, wisdom, and discernment should go together.[14]

---

[14] I have not considered, in this last section, where IS the afterlife, from which the discarnate allegedly communicate, and its relationship to our material world of three dimensions of space and one of time. That is beyond my remit and well beyond my capacity. Those who are interested in such matters will find useful information and insights in Becker (1993: 165–188), Carr (2008: 44–75), Oram (1998: 35–92), and Targ (2012: 209–216).

PART 3

Conclusions

Throughout this search I have been buffeted by a range of emotions and needs and it has been difficult to hold them all in balance. At the most visceral there has been a longing on the part of myself, Anne, and Dan to believe in the continued existence of Ralph and that he was safe, secure, and not suffering (against all the apparent daily evidence to the contrary that consciousness and personality are totally dependent on the body). There has also been the nagging fear of being deceived either by others or myself. I want Ralph to have survived. I have an intuition at my core that the world is not meaningless and that only some form of survival and development can make sense of it all. But, perhaps even deeper than this, I also have the animal desire for survival and the fear of extinction, and am acutely aware of the fearful and cowardly aspects in my own personality. For these reasons I have tried hard to adopt a critical and balanced approach to the evidence, and to inform myself of as much of the relevant historical and current anecdotal and research literature as I can. I freely admit that that is mainly English and American because it is the most easily available to me. The reader who wants a wider perspective from other cultures can consult the many articles of Carlos Alvarado easily accessible on the internet. I do not believe, finally, that I have been mentally unbalanced and deranged by grief and that this has affected my judgment. I do not hallucinate or hear voices, and the narrative of mild paranoia I described earlier, if anything, just sharpened my resolve to be as accurate and scrupulous in examining the evidence as I could.

So, with that preamble, I sum up. I have set myself four tasks. Firstly, to do a final reality check on our experiences. Secondly, to state my conclusions based on the eight assessment criteria outlined earlier. Thirdly, to identify a number of possible areas for development and enquiry in the systematic study of mediums. And finally, some words addressed to those parents, children, friends, or lovers who have found themselves in the same situation as Anne and myself.

There were three types of phenomena we experienced: physical phenomena in the early months and years after Ralph's death; the verbal information provided by mental mediums (the vast body of which was recorded so that we could avoid the error of memory slips and could review and review the material again and again at our leisure); and the intuitive, spontaneous sense of Ralph's presence in the house and his vivid appearances in my dreams in the first years after his death. I am afraid, doing the kind of reality check that Smith (2010) recommends in his critical book on the paranormal, I have to largely discount items one and three. Research on the internet eventually led me to discovering that long-life light bulbs occasionally behaved in the way I described in the text. However, it did not explain the precision of the timing and the sheer power of the discharge on occasions. Sadly, the sense of his presence in the house, by proxy in cigarette smoke, and in my dreams, no matter how vivid and consoling all this might be, had to be put aside as possible examples of magical thinking. There was also the danger that once one started to share experiences of this nature, other individuals and groups would reinforce this tendency, in what Taylor has called a process of reality drift (2004: 41–43). I particularly noticed this characteristic in the mediumship training session I attended and in discussions with bereaved individuals who talked about signs that their loved one was still communicating—*watch for bird feathers, that's a sign.* I kept spotting them for days and weeks after that conversation!

Therefore, I have to base my conclusions on the records and the analysis of those records of the ten sittings with mediums between 2002 and 2010 (I deliberately limited the number of sittings to prevent over-dependence clouding my judgment). That information was passed on which was accurate and not known to the medium is highly likely. See the assessment comments after the end of each reading. That some of that information was highly specific and virtually impossible to research is also highly probable: the whole first session was one string of detailed, precise, personal items, being spilled out rapidly one after the other. Two sittings were mediocre and the remainder good or better. However, though quite a lot of the information was at a generalised level, there were few crude examples of fishing and only one egregious attempt to turn false statements into accurate ones, by a verbal device (medium 10). Such tricks, while making one suspicious, should not be allowed to invalidate the total encounter. It is quite possible that a genuine and experienced medium resorts to a little padding or fishing to help them when the connection or their energy fades. A sympathetic recognition of this is not harmful. It is the quality of the overall evidence that is important.

I also think it remarkable that in eight out of the ten sittings (with different mediums except on one occasion) over nine years, the two people that I would most want to come through—Ralph and my father—did, either together or singly, and in ways that were characteristic of their beliefs, appearance, and histories. The sessions were also remarkably consistent about my character, situation, and interests. This is, surely, a form of replication. Can one possibly argue that eight cold reading mediums were so skilled and consistent that they could work to virtually identical scripts even though the sittings were separated in time and geography? It is also worth comment that so few actual errors were made.

One would expect the fraudulent medium to generate, occasionally, a number of quite spectacular own goals.

My research into the literature on the best mediums of the past and near present, and in the wider field of paranormal phenomena, strongly suggests to me that consciousness may not be totally dependent on the brain. Although this material is contentious, the sheer bulk of it is very impressive, given the very little funding available for its investigation and recording; and the case histories and the research go on. We are not dealing with a largely historical phenomenon. It seems to me that we need to continue to accumulate such evidence and to concentrate on the research and training questions about the creation of best conditions for the production of best evidence. I can see the attractions of trying to gain support from particular interpretations of quantum theory which might indicate that we live in a universe in which such things are possible. But there are dangers here. It would be unwise to discredit good evidence for survival by prematurely linking it to an application and expansion of quantum theory that many, even those strongly in favour of a spiritual and religious dimension, consider highly speculative.

As the readings mounted up over the years, I wondered what they actually said about the afterlife, as opposed to what was available from the wider literature. This was a disappointing area of enquiry. The sittings contained virtually nothing—except banalities or unverifiable statements —about the nature of the personality's continued existence. Ralph was becoming a healer, my father had his sisters around him and was getting to know his own father (true in the sense that in life he had rarely gone back his native Irish roots and had taken elocution lessons to divest himself of his broad Ulster accent), my mother-in-law was surrounded by roses, and Ralph was getting her a cup of tea. Please. I noticed, however, in my final review of the tapes that more had been said, *en passant*, about the nature of the afterlife than I had originally spotted. However, I have not added this material as it was just the usual generalised description that one could find in any popular Spiritualist publication, and I did not want to fall into the trap that I believe (and I stress this is only my personal opinion) that K. Paul Stoller fell into when he passed on 'communications' from his deceased son Galen in *My Life after Life: a Posthumous Memoir*. Stoller is a qualified doctor with a distinguished medical pedigree, but the book has virtually no evidential value and the description of the afterlife reads like science fantasy. I have great sympathy for his loss (as I have for all those personal accounts I have cited in this text or in the bibliography). But, again, the emphasis must always be on evidence.

My conclusions in terms of areas for future research are these. I believe the argument that mediums can access information from anomalous sources has been won, partly based on the evidence of the great trance mediums Mrs Piper, Mrs Leonard, and Mrs Garrett, and on the increasingly tight controls introduced in recent years (Beischel *et al.*). However, mediums in the Spiritualist traditions, and particularly mental mediums, have been investigated much less thoroughly. There is a real need to concentrate on the best mental mediums, from whatever tradition, and to work with them to improve their performance (it is interesting how fitful and staccato and bitty communications can be sometimes) with individual sitters. Parallel comparative work should also take place with instrumental transcommunication and with physical mediumship (provided full control protocols can be put in place) to see if there are similar underlying processes. There seems to be very little, if any, work of this nature. This is an absolutely crucial point since the converging evidence supportive of survival, reviewed above, tends to be irredeemably indirect, no matter how powerful and well corroborated. We have just not concentrated sufficiently on our best resource — the high quality mental medium.

The research and training and development should be underpinned by the extensive work that has been done (in the world of education and training) on the reception and decoding of information from the sensory modalities and on the valuing of experiential and work-based learning. It is vital for researchers and trainers to listen to mediums, sitters, and the alleged discarnates (a hugely unexplored territory). They are equal partners in the process. It is also crucial that a mechanism for transferring recent research into altered states of consciousness (Cardena and Winkelman, 2011) — the *know that* — is developed to help practising mediums with insights to help improve their own process — the *know how*. However, the research, training, and certification functions need to be firmly separated. It is quite possible (through no conscious intent on either side) for the need for certification to bias the information the medium provides the researcher.

On a broader front, initiatives with the major Spiritualist organisations in the United States and United Kingdom could bear substantial fruit: firstly, through cooperation between researchers and Spiritualists to devise high quality training programmes; and secondly, through systematic efforts to get copies, verbal and ideally visual when that happens, of a selection of the thousands of sittings that take place over the years, and to analyse them both for evidence of survival and for insight into process. I shudder to think of the high quality evidence that might have been lost in the past. It will be difficult to devise appropriate protocols and to sort out all the logistics, but with good will it can be done. The crucial point is to make the Spiritualist movements, the individual sitters, and the mediums full and equal partners, with equal control and status in all decision-making and activities. There are many interesting phenomena worth examining, but the basic experience of mental mediumship on a one-to-one basis is sorely under-researched and neglected, and yet it is probably the most common shared experience that people interested in the paranormal have —

the consultation with psychic or medium. And though it logically appears almost impossible to break the super-psi vs. individual survival logjam, the building up of more and more detailed evidence which carries the stamp of identity, planning, and purpose, and, as Beischel has indicated, establishes that psychic and mediumistic processes, while utilising the same 'forces', feel intuitively quite different to the mediums, may take us as close as we can get in this life to a solution.

Finally, a plea for realism and quality. Both Mrs Piper and Mrs Leonard had their incomes secured largely through the Society for Psychical Research. Mrs Piper probably over-sat and there is some evidence that her sittings were affected by this. Mrs Leonard sat less frequently, often only once a day, and carefully watched her diet and her general health. Modern mental mediums, in order to earn any kind of living, also risk over-sitting and, if they do platform work as well, have all the stresses that involves. We need a concentrated research programme with adequate funding to relieve the remarkable individuals concerned of financial worry for the time period involved.

So, what is my conclusion? And this I largely address to all those who have suffered a bereavement and who are wondering whether it is worth going to a medium. The experiences have had a very powerful healing effect on both Anne and me, particularly the first sitting. However, others can become over-dependent on mediums, particularly the psychologically naïve and those who have no background knowledge of this field. It is important to do preliminary reading and preparation, to have a positive but balanced and alert attitude at the sitting, and to be aware that such encounters can create their own authoritative enchantment, yet provide no real evidence. I learned from my possibly paranoid experiences of the ways in which we can all project significant meaning onto apparently trivial and partial stimuli. We seem built to fill the picture out with our own concerns and presuppositions.

And this may be so for the mediums too. They certainly can access information from non-sensory channels, but their Spiritualist interpretation is only one of a number of ways the sitting and the evidence can be read — and the more they are successful, and the more they and their community use that language, the more they will play that role and believe in the source of their information, as I temporarily did in my two moments of social anxiety outlined above. For example, I received much highly specific evidence, but none that was invulnerable to the super-psi hypothesis. So my final verdict does not rest on the emotion and power of the two most impressive sittings (1 and 9), but ultimately on my examination of the recorded material and on my wider reading. Based on that (heart locked in tussle with head) I'd have to use Sam Goldwyn's words when asked if he was going to turn a particular film script into a film,

It's a definite maybe.

Postscript

I thought I had experienced all I could and said all I wanted to say, but as this book was going through the press, I received, in emails on April 9th and 10th 2012, two long messages, apparently from Ralph, and transmitted by a medium to whom I had sent a draft of my book for comment. I had had a long series of emails on the nature of mediumship and training with this individual, and I respected them for their intelligence, balance, and obvious integrity. On receipt of the book they immediately began to experience contact with Ralph even though I had no intention of requesting a distance reading (it was not really appropriate and was also unfair) and they had a policy of not offering such a service. I should also stress that they thought the material had little evidential value but that they felt it ought to be sent anyway. I enclose some extracts:

(a) Medium

'I must also add, that much against my personal inclination, indeed quite strong opposition I have felt again several times today the presence of what I can only assume is your son... I was finally obliged to record a further message, especially after each time I tried to read your work the computer closed down.'

(b) Ralph

'I made [the medium] stop reading your work. I didn't want [them] to know too much about me or it would make it impossible for me to transmit any information through [their] mind.'

'in some respects I was beginning to get it together wasn't I? But then again, I wasn't all that sure in my mind whether I was going to make it. Don't be offended. In a way, going out that night was an acting out. A bit of recklessness before "knuckling down" to being serious about life. But I lost it. Went too far, and in the morning I felt pretty hopeless and annoyed with myself. I tried to shrug it off, made jokes, made light of everything, and decided to go home. When I got in the car I had the strangest feeling that I shouldn't but shrugged the thought off.'

'Working like this, as I am at the moment is hard. [The medium] is, at least, willing to listen to me, and to write my words down as I say them. Most of the others, Dad, were, to put it crudely, a "bit thick" when it came to trying to communicate. I would stand there beside them and end up feeling like I was shouting to get their attention and they missed most of it every time.'

(c) Medium

'The first message was written when I had not read any of the written material. The second was after having read to the beginning of page 5 when the computer went down. Each time I restarted and got near to Part 1, the computer closed down. Initially I thought it was just my computer being difficult... But... I found that looking at other things the computer did not fail.'

'The persistence, determination to get what was wanted and the sense of humour, complete with the most cheeky grin and wry smile is now very familiar to me.'

I found much of the material that was alleged to have come from Ralph very moving, and felt it was almost as if he had managed to break through at last, in a more coherent way, to express his love for us, his regrets, his philosophy of life, and the difficulties of communicating through mediums. But hard evidence, alas, it was not.

However, the medium who passed on the emails about Ralph also pointed out that my obsessive emphasis on verifiable material might lead me to miss matters of more general significance in terms of guidance, purpose, motivation, and support. And s/he was right. As I took a last glance at Appendix 2 on Predictive Statements, I realised I had missed something fundamental. The first six sittings had very little of a predictive nature — only 4. Whereas the last four sittings contained 52. It was as if there was a deliberate shift from proof of identity by the discarnates to support and encouragement for my aims and objectives in this terrestrial world. That is one interpretation. At the very least it will be interesting to see how much or how little of all this pans out and, at least, the predictions, in the best spirit of the Society for Psychical Research, have been committed to paper in advance of their possible fulfilment or not, as the case may be.

APPENDIX 1

Analysis of Results

Sitting	True	False	Other	Prediction	Total	Percent Correct
1	56	0	9	1	66	85
2	46	1	4	0	51	90
3	34	2	6	1	43	79
4	47	2	6	1	56	84
5	51	0	23	1	75	68
6	57	4	14	0	75	76
7	88	9	22	25	144	61
8	15	6	13	5	39	38
9	56	4	10	7	77	73
10	43	7	20	15	85	51

It should be noted, as I pointed out in the text, that a number of these statements could apply to many people, and that it is only in their selection, organization, and focus that they are impressive. However, a significant amount were very precise, and I find guessing, cold reading, etc. not persuasive in those situations. I have tried to identify where the medium may have used a spraying technique — that is, making several statements/questions rapidly in the hope that one of them will hit the target. But I have found very few examples of these: for example

Problems with her heart,
Breathing problems,
Pleurisy?

If fulfilled predictions were added in it would only make a real difference to sitting 7 and sitting 10, since these were the two mediums who seemed most to go in for that sort of thing. I have not bothered to do so as I find that part of mediumship highly dubious.

Appendix 1: Analysis of Results

In addition, it is often argued (Lyons & Truzzi, 1991: 154-55) that many apparently true statements are only true because they have 'multiple end points'. For example, the statement that a medium sees a body near water—many things would fit that. There is the further argument put forward to explain apparently precise hits—the law of large numbers. Given thousands of mediums have thousands of sittings with thousands of clients, and each time make hundreds of statements, some of them, sometimes, are bound occasionally to get something really spectacularly and specifically right. I would accept that a fair percentage of the statements I have recorded fall into the 'multiple end points' category but by no means all. As to the law of large numbers—at least two of the ten mediums (1 and 7) made several very precise and unambiguous assertions. One might plausibly be able to invoke that law on one occasion. But once, twice, thrice, etc. and with regard to different specific statements? It sounds a little desperate.[15]

---

[15] I accept that phrases like *I have to say three roses* or *There is a man you are comfortable with and whom you talk to* on one level can make one wince. Yet both those statements (for reasons which are far too complicated to go into) have a particular resonance for me. Are such statements just part of the repertoire of the skilled cold reader or are they attempts by the medium, under difficult conditions, to feel their way towards the communicator's message? Yet to push for further clarification, sometimes though not always, can lead to a breaking of the connection.

APPENDIX 2

Predictive Statements and their Status

Medium	Statement	Status
1	Parents not to worry re inquest. They won't be affected	True
2	None	
3	Don't give up. Just listen for one word – father	I did give up since nothing was happening
4	Your past ability will help you deal with things	It did, but this applies to many people
5	You will get your book published	I did
6	None	
7	She assures you, you will always have enough	This is just standard reassurance
	Finances better in 2008	Marginally
	You will be going to Spain	We did, but so did millions of people
	At 68 you will be more chilled out	Not in my nature to be chilled out, but I have become marginally less nervy
	You have it in you to achieve as a writer	Standard encouragement
	All in all five manuscripts by five years from now	There are five, of various types and lengths, now in the public domain
	You have got the ability	Again, standard reassurance or confidence building
	You will be published and successful	Published, yes, but success is quite another matter
	There are links to Yorkshire	We later went to Yorkshire, but so did hundreds of thousands of people
	You, too, will conquer in what you want to do	Yes, in that I have achieved my original goals

Appendix 2: Predictive Statements & their Status

	Statement	Status
	He is proud that you will be a noted author	'Noted author' is typical of the exuberant phrasing of this medium
	You have things to achieve and you still have time to do it	Again, generalised reassurance
	You have just got to write. It will flow	As above
	You will achieve	As above
	Success in later life is more appreciated and savoured	As above
	It is already a done deal he thinks	As above
	Lake Como will have spiritual significance for you in the future	We will see
	And have a lot of good things to achieve	More generalised morale building and exhortation
	You have so much to say. Release it	As above
	Your work will be easy to translate into film, to radio	One future project might be, but not all my work
	You can paint pictures with words	More exuberant flattery from this medium
	They wouldn't waste time pushing you if you didn't know how to write	As above
	You will have more than enough for all your needs	Generalised reassurance
	There is still a market for interesting work	General, vague encouragement, and how does he/they know?
	There is a link with this name [Jane] and the publishing of your books	This at least is specific, but she has not yet put in an appearance
8	You will be encountering people with unusual gifts	True. I have encountered a wide variety of people claiming a range of gifts
	Your destiny is to teach and talk and to instruct others	Again, this is highfalutin. I have given presentations — hardly earth-shattering!
	You have a lot to share with humanity	As above
	Travel to different countries	Yes, America. But not India as she suggested in the sitting
	You will be very successful	Only in the narrow sense of achieving limited goals
9	Very important for you [reference the possible image re cross-correspondences]	Both the timing and the nature of the image were very appropriate
	You have a vast knowledge which	Again, the generalised

	you need to share	exhortation/flattery associated with this field
	There is a connection to America work/business which is building	True
	There are good things to come from your work	General confidence building
	What you have wanted is coming	As above
	You will have a period of sharp pains in your ears	I did
	Also a whistling sound/watch out for it	I did. A curious experience as I described earlier
10	See you in suit/must be something coming	Piffle and just not true
	3 suits in closet	As above. I gave up suits a number of years ago
	Written a book/many more things to come and to do	True
	2nd trip to America/bestest time of your life	True, save for the hyperbole
	Interesting results	As above
	Mediumship/healing power building up in you	No evidence of this
	Noises in house in future	Piffle
	Due for optician	Trite and obvious
	Need to check teeth	As above
	You are going to be a busy, busy man	Busy, but not busy, busy
	She wants you to/you will be making a documentary	I had already briefly tried
	Pleasing results with documentary	There are some speculative plans, but I do not anticipate success
	When going no stopping you	I do have drive and energy when things interest me but so do many people
	More doorways opening	One or two, of a limited nature. But all this is very general
	One in South Africa	No sign of this

I think a passage from Oliver Lodge (1909: 161) is very relevant here: 'During the lifetime of Professor Sidgwick and Mr Myers we often discussed what sort of evidence could be regarded as conclusive as to the existence of supernormal, even if not posthumous, intelligence. And it was agreed that prediction of future events of an insignificant kind, such as could not be inferred or deduced by however wide a knowledge of contemporary events —

incidents which were outside the range of any amount of historical or mathematical or political skill, — would be conclusive, if obtained in quantity sufficient to eliminate chance.' I do not find any of the predictions concerning me to fall into that category. Some of them appeared to be low-level psychic counselling, while others seemed to be easily derived from the context.

The only things that have really impressed me of this nature were (a) the casual drop-in sitting with the very first medium who stated that there was a burden coming but I would bear it, that a red-headed woman would be significant, and that I would come into a lump sum, (b) the strange premonition outside Ralph's room that he would die and I would write about it, (c) the shattering and uneasy dream about a man in a wheelchair (the first medium) that I was afraid of and, in the same dream, linked to the vivid African mask which I later saw in the Pompidou Centre in Paris just before Ralph's death. But, I appreciate how, with retrospective emotional colouring, I can easily rearrange these things to give me meaning.

APPENDIX 3

Glossary

Note: these are very brief outline descriptions and purely intended as an initial introduction to highly complex concepts. Other terms are explained in the text and aspects of some of those mentioned here are elaborated in greater detail there.

Altered States of Consciousness (ASC). This refers to the different forms of consciousness experienced by individuals and often associated with a paranormal experience: trance, a hypnotic state, dreaming, etc.

Anomalous. An incident or experience which cannot be explained by current knowledge.

Astral Body. This is one of the finer, more subtle bodies that the spirit is supposed to inhabit after death. The others are the mental and the spiritual. Sometimes the term **etheric** is used, and there is some confusion in Spiritualist and occult literature as to the precise use of these and related terms. It is said that in an **out of body (OBE)** experience and in clairvoyance, it is the astral body that is projected to gather information. Out of body experiences can be spontaneous or intentional. Though in **remote viewing** where an individual's consciousness expands to gain access to a remote target, projection may not be the process whereby information is accessed.

Aura. This is a multi-coloured, sometimes called egg-shaped, energy field that is said to surround the body. Its identification, measurement, and relationship to the subtle bodies mentioned above is highly contested and problematic, as is the existence of subtle bodies themselves.

Automatic Writing. The unconscious and involuntary production of written material which may or may not have a source beyond the subconscious of the individual writing it. This is a particular example of **automatism**, which refers to a physical or mental activity not consciously initiated or produced by the individual concerned. Automatic drawing, painting, speaking, moving are also known.

Blind. Refers to individuals involved in experiments being kept ignorant of some or all aspects of the process in order to avoid leakage or bias. In mediumship research it is **single blind** if the medium does not know who the sitter is; **double blind** if neither medium nor sitter know who is reading for whom; and **triple blind** if the researchers are equally ignorant.

Clairvoyance. The gaining of information about an object or events through a process of paranormal vision. Mediums can be **clairvoyant**—seeing images; **clairaudient**—hearing voices; and **clairsentient**—working through feelings and intuitions. Or a mixture of all three.

Cosmic Data Base. This is a theory similar to the occult Akashic records doctrine that everything that has happened is stored in some permanent form and can be accessed under certain circumstances. This is linked to the **super-psi** hypothesis. See below.

Crystal Gazing. A technique used for centuries to see visions in a reflective surface—crystal, glass ball, etc.

Direct Voice. This is when the voice of an alleged spirit communicator is heard at a sitting with a medium, apparently not coming from the medium's voice box.

Drop-in Communicator. A communicator at a sitting who comes uninvited and is not known to those present.

fMRI. The scanning of the brain through Magnetic Resonance Imaging (**MRI**) while particular brain functions/activities/tasks are taking place (**f**).

Ganzfeld. This refers to a process of sensory deprivation where the eyes of the subject are covered and white noise is played in the ears. Such a condition is supposed to encourage a mildly altered state of consciousness which is particularly conducive to telepathy and possibly other phenomena.

Instrumental Transcommunication (ITC). A term used to describe the efforts of the deceased to communicate by sound or sight using technology—television, phone calls, radios, etc. It is said that this method does not require mediumistic gifts, but some of those involved clearly have had some psychic capacity. **EVP (Electronic Voice Production),** the capturing of allegedly discarnate voices on tape, comes within this category. It was one of the first forms of ITC to be initiated and noticed.

Incarnate—the living. **Discarnate**—the dead. It is a significant philosophical issue as to what extent one can talk meaningfully about identity when the discarnate are without a central feature of identity—a physical body.

Interactionism. One of the main perspectives on the mind/body relationship. It states that mind and body interact with each other and mutually influence each other; as opposed to **Cartesian dualism** where mind and body run on separate tracks and do not impact on each other; **physical monism** which asserts that all phenomena are ultimately physical and hence reduce to the laws of physics; which in turn is opposed to **mental monism** which argues that ultimately all is mind.[16]

Kirlian Photography. A supposed photographic record of the energy body (see **aura**) surrounding the individual. A technique developed by the Russian scientist Kirlian.

Magical Thinking. It is easy, particularly in a state of bereavement, depression, or stress, to attribute non-rational causes to events and

---

[16] Colborn (2011: 283) has argued that efforts to reduce these phenomena to any kind of monism is both constrictive and possibly futile. 'Let us learn to love the difference.'

incidents and to see paranormal patterns in life where none actually exists.

Medium. An individual capable of communicating with the dead, either in a complete state of trance or in a less complete altered state of consciousness. Other terms used are **sensitive** or **automatist**. This latter term emphasises the state of **dissociation** that the individual might be in: the hand writes as if controlled by a centre of consciousness not the medium's own. In full trance mediumship a medium may demonstrate personality traits and characteristics similar to (but not necessarily the same as) a **multiple personality disorder**.

Near-Death Experience (NDE). An experience at the point of death, or great threat and trauma, when individuals have a sense of being out of their body, moving down a tunnel or corridor to the light, sometimes encountering deceased friends and family, sometimes perceiving events in the physical environment although they are deeply unconscious, and often accompanied by a feeling of transcendence, peace, and security.

Pareidolia. The reading of meaning and significance into an apparently random natural object: the man in the moon, for example.

Parapsychology. The academic and scientific study of the paranormal by psychologists who tend to emphasise laboratory and experimental work on specific features or variables associated with the field—personality traits, environmental features, techniques. The older term **psychical research** tends to refer to those researchers who focus on spontaneous cases which rely on historical and documentary evidence. But the distinction is not absolute.

Psi. This is the general term used to refer to the underpinning force that causes paranormal phenomena. Sometimes called extra sensory perception (**ESP**) when referring to **clairvoyance** and **telepathy**, and sometimes called **psychokinesis** when there is a physical impact on the environment. **Super-psi** is the theory that, as we have no idea as to the capacities and boundaries of psi, it might well be that the evidence for the survival of bodily death could be equally adequately interpreted as evidence of the psychic powers of the living: that is **precognitive** (future) and **retrocognitive** (past) clairvoyance and telepathy can explain the acquisition of all the medium's information without recourse to the concept of a discarnate source.

Poltergeist. Literally noisy spirit. Strange noises, breakages, sometimes water deposits, sometimes fires, occurring in a house and attributed to the energies (usually) of adolescents or sometimes spirits.

Proxy Sittings. In order to prevent the medium gaining clues from the sitter's body language, etc. a volunteer (who knows nothing or very little about the real sitter) will sit with a medium on behalf of someone else.

Promnesia. Coined and defined by Myers as 'The paradoxical sensation of recollecting a scene which is only now occurring for the first time: the sense of *déjà vue*.'

Psychokinesis (PK). The ability of the psychic factor or force to make an impact on the physical environment. It is macro pk if the effect is clearly observable. It is micro pk if the use of statistics is needed to demonstrate its presence.

Reductive. Ultimately reduced to and explained by the laws of physics.

Reincarnation. The theory that the self or some part of the self is reborn after death into another body. A process which continues until the spirit is purified and has learnt all it needs to learn from earthly existence. The concept has often been explored through **hypnotic age regression**, where an individual has been taken back to childhood and beyond into an alleged previous existence.

Shaman. A tribal priest, often living isolated from the main group, whose practices and exercises enable them to contact the spirit world for the benefit of their community.

Subliminal. A term used by Myers to emphasise the fact that much psychic experience occurs below the level (below the sub limen, the threshold) of conscious thought.

Telepathy. Feeling at a distance. A term invented by Myers in 1882 to describe acquiring information from someone else other than through the normal sensory channels.

Veridical. This term was first used by Myers and his colleagues in connection with hallucinations. Hallucinations are delusive when there is nothing external to which they correspond, but veridical if they can be confirmed by real events happening elsewhere. The term—ugly but useful—now tends to be extended to any paranormal event that can be corroborated by external independent observation and documentation.

Resources and References

Websites and Blogs

Academic websites (the first is a small, independent organisation) studying mediumship and other paranormal phenomena include: www.windbridge.org, www.medicine.virginia.edu (division of perceptual studies), and www.koestler-parapsychology.psy.ed.ac.uk (Edinburgh University). The British (www.spr.ac.uk) and the American (www.aspr.com) societies for psychical research disseminate a range of information about the paranormal without espousing a collective view for or against. Two websites with strongly sceptical orientations are www.skepdic.com and www.csicop.org. Websites taking a pro, though evidence-based approach to the paranormal are www.paranormal.com (the website of Roy Stemman, a very experienced journalist in the field) and www.aeces.info (Association for Evaluation and Communication of Evidence of Survival). In a category all of its own is Victor Zammit's website, www.victorzammit.org, which, while strongly, humanely, and pugnaciously pro-survival (and at times credulously?), does provide a conduit to a vast amount of relevant information. Two websites that provide evidence for the highly contentious phenomenon of physical mediumship are www.circleofthesilvercord.net and www.felixcircle.blogspot.com.

The blogs of Michael Prescott, Dean Radin, James Randi, R.T. Carroll, Richard Wiseman, and Robert Mcluhan, easily accessible through a search engine, provide an entertaining and stimulating range of perspectives.

References

As an introduction to the different sides of the debate on the paranormal, I would particularly recommend the books by Mcluhan and by Wiseman. Other examples of those who, like Anne and I, came to it through personal loss, are the books by Byrne, Ireland, Kennedy, Picardie, Remmers, Rose, Stoller, and Swain. They tell their stories from their own highly individual viewpoints and backgrounds.

Allison, L.W. (1929) *Leonard and Soule Experiments in Psychical Research. Also Experiments with Sanders, Brittain, Peters and Dowden*, Boston, MA: Boston Society for Psychic Research.

Almeder, R. (1992) *Death and Personal Survival*, Lanham, MD: Littlefield Adams.

Alvarado, C.S. (2002) Dissociation in Britain during the late nineteenth century: The Society for Psychical Research 1882–1900, *Journal of Trauma and Dissociation*, 3: 9–33.

Alvarado, C.S. (2009) James H. Hyslop and the pictographic process in mediumistic communications, *Paranormal Review*, 49: 3–7.

Alvarado, C.S. (2011) On doubles and excursions from the physical body 1876–1956, *Journal of Scientific Exploration*, 25: 563–580.

Anderson, R.I. (2006) *Psychics, Sensitives and Somnambules. A Biographical Dictionary with Bibliographies*, Jefferson, NC: McFarland.

Angoff, A. (2009) *Eileen Garrett and the World Beyond the Senses*, New York: Helix Press.

Askwith, B. (1973) *Two Victorian Families*, London: Chatto & Windus.

Assagioli, R. (1993) *Psychosynthesis. A Manual of Principles and Techniques*, London: The Aquarian Press.

Augustine, K. (2012) http://www.infidels.org/library/modern/keith_augustine/immortality.html/ [accessed 09/03/2012].

Bargh, J.A. & Morsella, E. (2008) The unconscious mind, *Perspectives on Psychological Science*, 3: 73–79.

Barrington, M.R. (1966) Swan on a black sea: How much could Miss Cummins have known?, *Journal of the Society for Psychical Research*, 43: 289–300.

Barrington, M.R. (2002) The Case of Jenny Cockell: Towards a verification of an unusual 'past life' report, *Journal of the Society for Psychical Research*, 66: 106–112.

Beard, P. (1992) *Inner Eye, Listening Ear. An Exploration into Mediumship*, Norwich: Pilgrim Books.

Beauregard, M. (2012) *Brain Wars. The Scientific Battle over the Existence of the Mind and the Proof That Will Change the Way We Live Our Lives*, New York: HarperOne.

Becher, T. & Trowler, P.R. (2001) *Academic Tribes and Territories*, Buckingham: Open University.

Becker, C.B. (1993) *Paranormal Experience and Survival of Death*, New York: State University Press.

Beischel, J. (2007) Contemporary methods used in laboratory-based mediumship research, *Journal of Parapsychology*, 71: 37–68.

Beischel, J. (2010) The reincarnation of mediumship research, *Edgescience*, 3: 10–12.

Beischel, J. & Rock, A.J. (2009) Addressing the survival versus psi debate through process-focused mediumship research, *Journal of Parapsychology*, 73: 71–90.

Bennett, M.R. & Hacker, P.M.S. (2003) *Philosophical Foundations of Neuroscience*, Oxford: Blackwell.

Berger, A.S. (1987) Foreword, Flew, A., *Aristocracy of the Dead. New Findings in Postmortem Survival*, Jefferson, NC: McFarland.

Berger, A.S. (2010) *Evidence of Life After Death. A Case Book for the Tough-Minded*, Aventura, FL: Survival Research Foundation.

Blackmore, S. (1997) Probability misjudgement and belief in the paranormal. A newspaper survey, *British Journal of Psychology*, 88: 683–699.

Boccuzzi, M. & Beischel, J. (2011) Objective analyses of reported real-time audio instrumental transcommunication and matched control sessions: A pilot study, *Journal of Scientific Exploration*, 25: 215–235.

Borgia, A. (1954) *Life in the World Unseen*, Foreword, Anderson, J., London: Odhams.

Botkin, A.L. & Hogan, R.C. (2005) *Induced After Death Communication. A New Therapy for Healing Grief and Trauma*, Charlottesville, VA: Hampton Roads.

Braude, S.E. (1992) Survival or super-psi?, *Journal of Scientific Exploration,* 6: 127–144.

Braude, S.E. (1995) *First Person Plural. Multiple Personality and the Philosophy of Mind,* Lanham, MD: Rowman and Littlefield.

Braude, S.E. (2003) *Immortal Remains: The Evidence for Life after Death,* Lanham, MD: Rowman and Littlefield.

Broad, C.D. (1925) *The Mind and its Place in Nature,* London: Kegan Paul.

Byrne, G. (1994) *Russell,* London: Janus Publishing.

Cardena, E. & Winkelman, M. (eds.) (2011) Preface, Tart, C.T., *Altering Consciousness: Multidisciplinary Perspectives, Vol. 1: History, Culture and the Humanities,* Westport, CT: Praeger.

Cardena, E. & Winkelman, M. (eds.) (2011) Preface, Pope, K.S., *Altering Consciousness: Multidisciplinary Perspectives, Vol. 2: Biological and Psychological Perspectives,* Westport, CT: Praeger.

Carpenter, J.C. (2012) *First Sight. ESP and Parapsychology in Everyday Life,* Lanham, MD: Rowman & Littlefield.

Carr, B. (2008) Worlds apart? Can psychical research bridge the gulf between matter and mind?, *Proceedings of the Society for Psychical Research,* 59: 1–96.

Cattanach, R. (2007) *Best of Both Worlds,* London: Pembridge.

Clarke, C. & King, M. (2006) Lazlo and McTaggart—in the light of this thing called physics, *Network Review,* Winter: 6–11.

Colborn, M. (2011) *Pluralism and the Mind. Consciousness, Worldviews and the Limits of Science,* Exeter: Imprint Academic.

Coleman, T. (2010) *The Afterlife Investigations,* DVD. See also http://www.timcoleman.tv

Collins, H.M. (1992) *Changing Order. Replication and Induction in Scientific Practice,* Chicago: University of Chicago Press.

Cook, E.W. (Kelly) (1996) Survival research today: An essay review of parapsychology and thanatology, *The Journal of Parapsychology,* 60: 343–355.

Cook, E.W. (Kelly), Greyson, B. & Stevenson, I. (1998) Do any near-death experiences provide evidence for the survival of human personality after death? Relevant features and illustrative case reports, *Journal of Scientific Exploration,* 12: 377–406.

Cornell, T. (2002) *Investigating the Paranormal*, New York: Helix Press.

Crookall, R. (1960) *The Study and Practice of Astral Projection*, London: The Aquarian Press.

Crookall, R. (1975) *The Supreme Adventure. Analyses of Psychic Communications*, London: James Clarke.

Cummins, G. (1951) *Unseen Adventures. An Autobiography Covering 34 Years of Psychic Research*, London: Rider.

Cummins, G. (1965) Toksvig, S. (ed.), Foreword, Broad, C.D., *Swan on a Black Sea*, London: Routledge.

Cummins, G. (1967) *The Road to Immortality*, London: Psychic Press.

Dobinson, G. (2001) Clairvoyance by telephone, *Paranormal Review*, 19: 10

Dodds, E.R. (1934) Why I do not believe in survival, *Proceedings of the Society for Psychical Research*, 135: 147–172.

Dodds, E.R. (1977) *Missing Persons. An Autobiography*, Oxford: Clarendon Press.

Ducasse, C.J. (1962) What would constitute conclusive evidence of survival after death?, *Journal of the Society for Psychical Research*, 41: 401–406.

Eagleman, D. (2011) *Incognito. The Secret Lives of the Brain*, London: Canongate.

Eisenbeiss, W. & Hassler, D. (2006) An assessment of ostensible communications with a deceased grandmaster as evidence for survival, *Journal of the Society for Psychical Research*, 70: 65–97.

Ellis, D.J. (1978) *The Mediumship of the Tape Recorder: A Detailed Examination of the (Jürgenson, Raudive) Phenomena of Voice Extras on Tape Recordings*, Pulborough: D.J. Ellis.

Ellison, A.J. (2002) *Science and the Paranormal. Altered States of Reality*, Foreword Fontana, D., Bristol: Floris.

Emmons, C.F. & Emmons, P. (2003) *Guided by Spirit. A Journey into the Mind of the Medium*, New York: Writers Club Press.

Farthing, G.W. (1992) *The Psychology of Consciousness*, Englewood Cliffs, NJ: Prentice Hall.

Fenwick, P. & Fenwick, E. (2008) *The Art of Dying. A Journey to Elsewhere*, London: Continuum.

Findlay, A.J. (1932) *On the Edge of the Etheric or Survival after Death Scientifically Explained*, Foreword Barrett, W., London: Rider.

Firebrace, R.H., Gay, K., et al. (1955) Report on the Oliver Lodge Posthumous Test, *Journal of the Society for Psychical Research*, 38: 121–134.

Flew, A. (1953) *A New Approach to Psychical Research*, London: Watts.

Fontana, D. (2005) *Is There an Afterlife? A Comprehensive Overview of the Evidence*, Winchester: O Books.

Fontana, D. (2009) *Life Beyond Death. What Should We Expect?*, London: Watkins.

Foy, R. (2008) *Witnessing the Impossible*, Diss: Torcal Publications.

Fuller, J.G. (1979) *The Airmen Who Would Not Die*, London: Souvenir Press.

Gardner, H. (1985) *Frames of Mind. The Theory of Multiple Intelligences*, London: Paladin.

Garland, H. (1939) *The Mystery of the Buried Crosses. A Narrative of Psychic Exploration*, New York: E.P. Dutton & Co.

Gauld, A. & Cornell, A.D. (1979) *Poltergeists*, London: Routledge & Kegan Paul.

Gauld, A. (1982) *Mediumship and Survival: A Century of Investigations*, London: Heinemann.

Gauld, A. (1998) Philosophy and survival: An essay review of R.W.K. Paterson's philosophy and the belief in life after death, *Journal of the Society for Psychical Research*, 62: 453–462.

Gilbert, H. (2007) The 31st SPR Annual Conference at Cardiff, *Paranormal Review*, 44: 27–29.

Goforth, A. (2011) The disparity of a 'standards of care' for spirit mediumship as a permissible behavioural health care profession, *Paranthology: Journal of Anthropological Approaches to the Paranormal*, 2: 65–91.

Grayling, A.C. (ed.) (2004) *Philosophy 1. A Guide Through the Subject*, Oxford: Oxford University Press.

Guirdham, A. (1974) *We Are One Another. A Record of Group Reincarnation*, Jersey: Neville Spearman.

Gustus, S. (2011) *Less Incomplete. A Guide to Experiencing the Human Condition Beyond the Physical Body*, Winchester: O Books.

Hacking, I. (2009) *An Introduction to Probability and Inductive Logic,* Cambridge: Cambridge University Press.

Hamilton, T. (2009) *Immortal Longings. FWH Myers and the Victorian search for Life after Death,* Exeter: Imprint Academic.

Hamilton, T.G. (1977) Hamilton, M.L. (ed.) *Intention and Survival. Psychical Research Studies and the Bearing of Intentional Actions by Trance Personalities on the Problem of Human Survival,* London: Regency Press.

Hamilton, M.L. (1969) *Is Survival a Fact? Studies of deep-trance automatic scripts and the bearing of intentional actions by the trance personalities on the question of human survival,* London: Psychic Press.

Harris, L. (2000) *The Cathars and Arthur Guirdham. An Investigation into the Past Lives of a Bath Psychiatrist and his Circle,* London: PsyPioneer.

Harris, Louie (2009) *Alec Harris. The Full Story of his Remarkable Physical Mediumship,* York: Saturday Night Publications.

Harrison, T. (2004) *Life After Death – Living Proof,* York: Saturday Night Publications.

Hart, H. (1959) *The Enigma of Survival. The Case For and Against an After Life,* London: Rider and Company.

Hatton, E. (2010) *Taking Up the Challenge,* Beaconsfield: Saturday Night Press.

Hick, J. (1976) *Death & Eternal Life,* London: Collins.

Hick, J. (2004) *The Fifth Dimension. An Exploration of the Spiritual Realm,* Oxford: Oneworld.

Heath, P.R. & Klimo, J. (2010) *Handbook to the Afterlife,* Berkeley, CA: North Atlantic Books.

Hodgson, D. (1995) Probability the logic of the law – a response, *Oxford Journal of Legal Studies,* 15: 51–68.

Holden, J.M., Greyson, B. & James, D. (eds.) (2009) *The Handbook of Near-Death Experiences. Thirty Years of Investigation,* Foreword Chopra, D., Santa Barbara, CA: Praeger.

Humphrey, N. (1996) *Soul Searching. Human Nature and Supernatural Belief,* London: Vintage.

Hunt, H.E. (1936) *Do We Survive Death?,* London: Rich and Cowan.

Hyman, R. (2003) How *not* to test mediums. Critiquing afterlife experiments, *Skeptical Inquirer*, Jan/Feb: 20–30.

Hyslop, J.H. (1901) A further record of observations of certain trance phenomena, *Proceedings of the Society for Psychical Research*, 16: 1–649.

Hyslop, J.H. (1919) *Contact with the Other World. The Latest Evidence as to Communication with the Dead*, New York: The Century Co.

Ireland, M. (2008) *Soul Shift. Finding Where the Dead Go*, Berkeley, CA: Frog Books.

Irwin, H.J. & Watt, C.A. (2007) *An Introduction to Parapsychology*, Jefferson, NC: McFarland.

Jahn, R.G. & Dunne, B.J. (2011) The uses and misuses of quantum jargon, *Journal of Scientific Exploration*, 25: 339–341.

James, W. (1986) Burkhard, F.W., Bowers, F. & Skrupskelis, I.K. (eds.) *Essays in Psychical Research*, Harvard, MA: Harvard University Press.

Kaplan, A. (1998) *The Conduct of Enquiry. Methodology for Behavioural Science*, Introduction Wolf, C., New Brunswick, NJ: Transaction.

Katra, J. (2011) http:// www.janekatra.org./docs/adcs_elisabeth_talk.pdf (accessed 23/9/2011).

Keene, M.L. & Spragg, A. (1976) *The Psychic Mafia*, Introduction Rauscher,W.V., New York: St Martin's Press.

Kelly, E. (2011) Review of 'Out-of-Body and Near-Death Experiences: Brain-state phenomena or glimpses of immortality?' by Michael N. Marsh, *Journal of Scientific Exploration*, 24: 729–737.

Kelly, E.F., Kelly, E.W., Crabtree, A., Gauld, A., Grosso, M. & Greyson, B. (2007) *Irreducible Mind. Towards a Psychology for the 21st Century*, Lanham, MD: Rowman and Littlefield.

Kelly, E.W. (2010) Some directions for mediumship research, *Journal of Scientific Exploration*, 24: 247–282.

Kelly, E.W. & Arcangel, D. (2011) An investigation of mediums who claim to give information about deceased persons, *The Journal of Nervous and Mental Diseases*, 1: 11–17.

Kennedy, D. (1974) *A Venture in Immortality*, Gerrards Cross: Colin Smythe.

Klimo, J. (1998) *Channeling. Investigations on Receiving Information from Paranormal Sources*, Foreword Tart, C.T., Berkeley, CA: North Atlantic Books.

Knight, D. (2004) *Science and Spirituality. The Volatile Connection*, London: Routledge.

Kolb, D.A. (1984) *Experiential Learning*, Upper Saddle River, NJ: Prentice Hall.

Krippner, S. & Friedman, H.L. (eds.) (2010) *Debating Psychic Experience. Human Potential or Human Illusion*, Foreword Richards, R., Santa Barbara, CA: ABC-CLIO.

LaGrand, L.E. (1997) *After Death Communications. Final Farewells*, Woodbury, MN: Llewellyn.

Lawton, D. (2010) The bodily survival of bodily death, *Scientific and Medical Network*, members archive.

Leininger, B., Leininger, A. & Gross, K. (2009) *Soul Survivor. The Reincarnation of a World War II Fighter Pilot*, London: Hay House.

Lodge, O. (1909) *The Survival of Man. A Study in Unrecognised Human Faculty*, London: Methuen.

Lyons, A. & Truzzi, M. (1991) *The Blue Sense. Psychic Detectives and Crime*, New York: Warner Books.

Mackian, S. (2010) In possession of my senses? Reflections from social science on engaging with the otherworldly, *Paranthology: Journal of Anthropological Approaches to the Paranormal*, 2: 27–29.

Manning, M. (1974) *The Link. The Extraordinary Gifts of a Teenage Psychic*, Gerrards Cross: Colin Smythe.

Manning, M. & Rose, T. (1999) *One Foot in the Stars. The Story of the World's Most Extraordinary Healer*, Shaftesbury: Element.

McGilchrist, I. (2009) The divided brain and the making of the western world, *Network Review*, Winter: 3–6.

Mcluhan, R. (2010) *Randi's Prize. What Sceptics Say about the Paranormal, Why they are Wrong & Why it Matters*, London: Matador.

Miller, J. (1986) *One Girl's War. Personal Exploits in MI5's Most Secret Station*, Kerry: Brandon.

Mills, A. & Dhiman, K. (2011) Shiva returned in the body of Sumitra: A posthumous longitudinal study of the significance of the Shiva/Sumitra case of the possession type, *Proceedings of the Society for Psychical Research*, 59: 145–193.

Montefiore, H. (2002) *The Paranormal. A Bishop Investigates*, Leicester: Upfront Press.

Moody, R., with Perry, P. (1993) *Reunions. Visionary Encounters with Departed Loved Ones*, New York: Villard Books.

Moreman, C.M. (2010) *Beyond the Threshold. Afterlife Beliefs and Experiences in World Religions*, Plymouth: Rowman and Littlefield.

Munday, R. (2003) *Evidence*, London: LexisNexis.

Murphy, M. (1992) *The Future of the Body. Explorations into the Further Evolution of Human Nature*, Los Angeles, CA: Tarcher.

Myers, F.W.H. & Barrett, W.F. (1889) Review of *D.D.Home, his Life and Mission* by Mme. Home, *Journal of the Society for Psychical Research*, 4: 101–136.

Myers, F.W.H. (1892) On indications of continued terrene knowledge on the part of phantasms of the dead, *Proceedings of the Society for Psychical Research*, 8: 170–252.

Myers, F.W.H. (1904) *Human Personality and Its Survival of Bodily Death*, 2 vols., London: Longmans.

Nickell, J. (1998) *A Case of Reincarnation-Reexamined*, http://www.csicop.org/sb/show/case/_of_reincarnation_reexamined/ (accessed 25/2/2012).

Nowotny-Keane, E. (2009) *Amazing Encounters. Direct Communication from the Afterlife*, Melbourne: David Lovell.

O'Keeffe, C. & Wiseman, R. (2005) Testing alleged mediumship. Methods and results, *British Journal of Psychology*, 96: 165–179.

Oram, A. (1998) *The System in Which We Live*, Purley: Talbot Books.

Osis, K. & Haraldsson, E. (1997) *At the Hour of Death*, Norwalk, CT: Hastings House.

Parra, A. & Villanueva, J. (2011) Mirror-gazing facility and psi: Examining personality measures, *Journal of the Society for Psychical Research*, 75: 177–190.

Paul, P. (2010) The curious case of Gordon Higginson, *Psypioneer*, 6: 136–146.

Peake, A. (2011) Foreword, Lazlo, E., *The Out of Body Experience. The History and Science of Astral Travel*, London: Watkins Publishing.

Perry, M. & Fontana, D. (2009) Charles Fryer and his tape, *Paranormal Review*, 52: 12–13.

Picardie, J. (2001) *If the Spirit Moves You. Life and Love after Death*, London: Macmillan.

Playfair, G.L., Keen, M. (2004) A possibly unique case of psychic detection, *Journal of the Society for Psychical Research*, 68: 1–17.

Playfair, G.L. (2010) *Chico Xavier. Medium of the Century*, London: Roundtable Publishing.

Powell, D.H. (2010) *The ESP Enigma. The Scientific Case for Psychic Phenomena*, New York: Walker.

Poynton, J. (2011) Science, politics and psychical research. Many levels, many worlds and psi: A guide to the work of Michael Whiteman. Michael Whiteman: A biographical sketch, *Proceedings of the Society for Psychical Research*, 59: 97–143.

Poynton, J. (2012) Review of Peake, A. (2011) Foreword, Lazlo, E., The Out of Body Experience. The History and Science of Astral Travel. London: Watkins Publishing, *Journal of the Society for Psychical Research*, 76: 116.

Price, H.H. (1953) Survival and the idea of 'another world', *Proceedings of the Society for Psychical Research*, 50: 1–25.

Price, L. et al. (2011) Fraudulent medium of the century?, *Psypioneer*, 7: 133–135, *et passim*.

Radin, D.I. & Rebman, J.M. (1996) Are phantasms fact or fantasy? A preliminary investigation of apparitions evoked in the laboratory, *Journal of the Society for Psychical Research*, 61: 65–87.

Remmers, J.H. (1967) *The Great Reality*, London: Spiritualist Press.

Rivas, T. (1991–2) Alfred Peacock? Reincarnation fantasies about the Titanic, *Journal of the Society for Psychical Research*: 10–15.

Roach, M. (2005) *Spook. Science Tackles the Afterlife*, New York: Norton.

Roberts, J. (1978) *The Afterdeath Journal of an American Philosopher. The World View of William James*, Englewood Cliffs, NJ: Prentice Hall.

Robertson, T.J. & Roy, A.E. (2001) A preliminary study of the acceptance by non-recipients of mediums' statements to recipients, *Journal of the Society for Psychical Research*, 65: 91–106.

Rock, A.J., Beischel, J. & Cott, C.C. (2009) Psi vs. survival: A qualitative investigation of mediums' phenomenology comparing psychic readings and ostensible communication with the deceased, *Transpersonal Psychology Review,* 13: 76–89.

Rogers, P., Davis, T. & Fisk, J. (2009) Paranormal belief and susceptibility to the conjunction fallacy, *Applied Cognitive Psychology,* 23: 524–542.

Roll, W. (1974) Survival research: Problems and possibilities, in Mitchell, E.D. & White, J. (eds.) *Psychic Exploration: A Challenge for Science,* 397–424, New York: Putnam.

Roney-Dougal, S. (2010) *Where Science and Magic Meet,* Dorchester: Green Magic.

Rose, A. (1997) *Journey into Immortality. The Story of David Rose,* Harpenden: Lennard Publishing.

Rousseau, D. (2011) Physicalism, Christianity and the Near-Death Experience: An essay review of 'Out-of-Body and Near-Death Experiences: Brain-State Phenomena or Glimpses of Immortality?' by Michael Marsh, *Journal of the Society for Psychical Research,* 75: 225–234.

Rousseau, D. (2012) The implications of Near-Death Experiences for research into the survival of consciousness, *Journal of Scientific Exploration,* 26: 43–80.

Rowland, I. (2002) *The Full Facts Book of Cold Reading,* London: Ian Rowland.

Roxborough, E.C. (2006) Mediumship, spirit awareness and developing your potential: A personal view of a course at the Arthur Findlay College, *Paranormal Review*: 18–23.

Roxborough, E.C., Roe, C.A., Rock, A.J., Beischel, J. & Schwartz, G.E. (2009) Letters on thematic analysis of mediums' experiences, *Journal of Scientific Exploration,* 23: 348–357.

Roy, A.E. & Robertson, T.J. (2001) A double-blind procedure for assessing the relevance of a medium's statement to a recipient, *Journal of the Society for Psychical Research,* 65: 161–174.

Roy, A.E. & Robertson, T.J. (2004) Results of the application of the Robertson-Roy protocol to a series of experiments with mediums and participants, *Journal of the Society for Psychical Research,* 68: 18–34.

Roy, A.E. (2008) *The Eager Dead. A Study in Haunting,* Foreword Wilson, C., Brighton: Book Guild Publishing.

Rubinstein, I.D. (2011) *Consulting Spirit. A Doctor's Experience with Practical Mediumship,* San Antonio, TX: Anomalist Books.

Salter, W.H. (1958) F.W.H. Myers' posthumous message, *Proceedings of the Society for Psychical Research,* 52: 1–32.

Saltmarsh H.F. & Soal, S.G. (1930-31) A method of estimating the supernormal content of mediumistic communications, *Proceedings of the Society for Psychical Research,* 39: 266–271.

Saltmarsh, H.F. (1975) *Evidence of Personal Survival From Cross Correspondences,* New York: Arno Press.

Schouten, S.A. (1994) An overview of quantitatively evaluated studies with mediums and psychics, *Journal of the American Society for Psychical Research,* 88: 221–254.

Schwartz, G.E. with Simon, W.L. (2002) *The Afterlife Experiments. Breakthrough Scientific Evidence of Life after Death,* New York: Pocket Books.

Schwartz, G.E. (2011) Foreword Chopra, D., *The Sacred Promise. How Science is Discovering Spirit's Collaboration with Us in Our Daily Lives,* New York: Atria.

Schwartz, J.M. & Begley, S. (2002) *Neuroplasticity and the Power of Mental Force. The Mind & The Brain,* New York: Harper.

Sidgwick, E. (1924) Review of the 'Oscar Wilde' script, *Proceedings of the Society for Psychical Research,* 34: 186–196.

Smith, J.C. (2010) *Pseudoscience and Extraordinary Claims of the Paranormal. A Critical Thinker's Toolkit,* Chichester: Wiley-Blackwell.

Smith, S. (1964) *The Mediumship of Mrs Leonard,* New York: University Books.

Smith, S. (2000a) *The Book of James (William James, That Is). Conversations from Beyond,* New York: toExcel.

Smith, S. (2000b) *The Afterlife Codes. Searching for Evidence of the Survival of the Soul,* Charlottesville, VA: Hampton Roads.

Smythies, J. (2000) The theoretical basis of psi, *Journal of the Society for Psychical Research,* 64: 242–244.

Solomon, G. & Solomon, J. (in association with the Scole Experimental Group) (1999) *The Scole Experiment. Scientific Evidence for Life after Death,* Foreword Ellison, A., London: Piatkus.

Stevenson, I. (1974) *Twenty Cases Suggestive of Reincarnation*, Charlottesville, VA: University of Virginia Press.

Stevenson, I. (1997) *Where Reincarnation and Biology Intersect*, Westport, CT: Praeger.

Stevenson, I. (1999) What are the irreducible components of the scientific enterprise?, *Journal of Scientific Exploration*, 13: 257–270.

Stevenson, I. (2003) *European Cases of the Reincarnation Type*, Jefferson, NC: McFarland.

Stevenson, I. (2008) Scientists with half-closed minds, *Journal of Scientific Exploration*, 22: 132–140.

Stokes, D.M. (1993) Mind, matter and death: Cognitive neuroscience and the problem of survival, *Journal of the American Society for Psychical Research*, 87: 41–84.

Stoller, G. (2011), Stoller, K.P. (ed.) *My Life After Life. A Posthumous Memoir*, Santa Fe, NM: Dream Treader Press.

Storm, L. & Rock, A.J. (2011) Foreword, Tressoldi, P.E., *Shamanism and Psi. Imagery Cultivation as an Alternative to the Ganzfeld Protocol*, Gladesville, NSW: Australian Institute of Parapsychological Research.

Sudduth, M. (2009) Super-psi and the survivalist interpretation of mediumship, *Journal of Scientific Exploration*, 23: 167–193

Swain, J. (1974) Foreword, Langley, N., *On the Death of My Son*, London: Turnstone Books.

Swanson, C. (2009) *The Synchronized Universe. New Science of the Paranormal*, Tucson, AZ: Poseidia Press.

Swanson, C. (2011) *Life Force, The Scientific Basis: Breakthrough Physics of Energy Medicine, Healing, Chi and Quantum Consciousness*, Tucson, AZ: Poseidia Press.

Swinburne, R. (2004) The possibility of life after death, in Cave, P. & Larvor, B. (eds.) *Thinking About Death*, 38–42, London: London British Humanist Association.

Targ, R. (2012) Foreword, Schwartz, S.A., *The Reality of ESP: A Physicist's Proof of Psychic Abilities*, Wheaton, IL: Quest Books.

Tart, C.T. (2009) *The End of Materialism. How Evidence of the Paranormal is Bringing Science and Spirit Together*, Oakland, CA: Noetic Books & New Harbinger Publications.

Taylor, K. (2004) *Brainwashing. The Science of Thought Control,* Oxford: Oxford University Press.

Thomas, J.F. & McDougall, W. (1937) *Beyond Normal Cognition: An Evaluative and Methodological Study of the Mental Content of Certain Trance Phenomena,* Boston, MA: Bruce Humphries Inc.

Tucker, J.B. (2011)Foreword, Stevenson, I., *Life Before Life. A Scientific Investigation of Children's Memories of Previous Lives,* London: Piatkus.

Tymn, M.E. (2008) *The Articulate Dead. They Brought the Spirit World Alive,* Lakeville, MN: Galde Press.

Tymn, M.E. (2011a) *The Afterlife Revealed. What Happens After We Die,* Guildford: White Crow Books.

Tymn, M.E. (2011b) *Transcending the Titanic. Beyond Death's Door,* Guildford: White Crow Books.

Utts, J. (1995) An assessment of the evidence for psychic functioning, *Journal of Parapsychology,* 59: 289–320.

Utts, J. (1999) The significance of statistics in mind-matter research, *Journal of Scientific Exploration,* 13: 615–638.

Vandersande, J.W. (2008) *Life After Death. Some of the Best Evidence,* Denver, CO: Outskirts Press.

Walker, E.H. (2000) *The Physics of Consciousness. Quantum Minds and the Meaning of Life,* Cambridge, MA: Perseus Publishing.

Walker, N. (1927) *The Bridge. A Case for Survival,* London: Cassell.

Walker, N. (1935) *Through a Stranger's Eyes. New Evidence for Survival,* London: Hutchinson.

White, S.E. (1969) *The Betty Book (Excursions into the World of Other-Consciousness),* London: Psychic Press.

Whiteman, J.H.M. (1986) *Old and New Evidence on the Meaning of Life. The Mystical World-View and Inner Contest. An Introduction to Scientific Mysticism,* Gerrards Cross: Colin Smythe.

Williams, B.J. (2011) Revisiting the Ganzfeld ESP debate: A basic review and assessment, *Journal of Scientific Exploration,* 25: 639–661.

Williams, B.O. (2010) Imaging the human energy field, *Edgescience,* 4: 17–19.

Wilson, I. (1987) *The After Death Experience,* London: Sidgwick & Jackson.

Wiseman, R. & Morris, R.L. (1995) *Guidelines for Testing Psychic Claimants,* New York: Prometheus Books.

Wiseman, R. (2011) *Paranormality. Why we see what isn't there,* London: Macmillan.

Wright, S.H. (2002) *When Spirits Come Calling. The Open-minded Skeptic's Guide to After-Death Contacts,* Foreword Greeley, A.M., Nevada City, CA: Blue Dolphin.

Youens, T. & Shaw, A. (2006) *Did a Medium Identify a Murderer?*, www.tonyyouens.com [accessed 21/08/2011].

Zeman, A. (2002) *Consciousness. A User's Guide,* Newhaven, CT: Yale University Press.